GILEAD NOW

TEN INGREDIENTS FOR HEALING A PAINFUL PAST

DEBBIE VANDERSLICE

WESTBOW°
PRESS
A DIVISION OF THOMAS NELSON
& ZONDERVAN

Author Credits: Previously published Shameless by New Hope Publishers
and The Walking Wounded by Cross Books

WestBow Press books may be ordered through booksellers or by contacting:

WestBow Press
A Division of Thomas Nelson & Zondervan
1663 Liberty Drive
Bloomington, IN 47403
www.westbowpress.com
1 (866) 928-1240

ISBN: 978-1-4908-7893-5 (sc)
ISBN: 978-1-4908-7894-2 (e)

Library of Congress Control Number: 2015906988

Print information available on the last page.

WestBow Press rev. date: 06/08/2015

A Women's In-Depth Bible Study

Gilead Now

10 Ingredients to Healing

Jeremiah 8:22 "Is there no balm in Gilead? Is there no physician there? Why then is there no healing for the wound of my people?" (NIV)

Gilead Now is a bible study that examines why we do not heal from wounds that have occurred and offers hope to healing a painful past.

Written by Debbie Vanderslice

DEDICATION

To all those who suffer from depression. I know your pain and struggles. May God be our Balm in Gilead

To: Hannah: you are the pride and joy of my life. I love you SO much sweet pea

To: Sherry: Thank you for believing in me through thick and thin

To: Leigh Anne: Thank you for being there during my darkest days

To: Martha Jane: Thank you for introducing me to The King of Kings and Lord of Lords

To: Ginny, Lisa, Kay, and Louise, Dana, the pastoral care team, and our congregation. Thank you beyond words.

(Interior Book) Gilead Now asks why so many Christians do not heal from a wounded life and offers ten ingredients to healing a difficult past. This bible study uses the scripture, Jeremiah 8:22 as the guiding force for parts one, two, and three.

(Dusk Jacket Text) Part one, *Healing the Past*, takes aim at discussing the different responsibilities we each have as believers. Part two, *Living in the Present*, zeroes in on how we must live in the present while never denying the past. Part three, *Yearning for the Future*, the key is on the hope we are to have as believers while living in the present and yet, never omitting the past.

It is the goal of *Gilead Now* to validate each reader's feelings in regard to her wounded past, while at the same time never denying the obstacles she must overcome in order to bring healing to her particular struggle.

My bible study is powerful, candid, and hopeful for millions and millions of Christian women who have been wounded in very specific ways and find themselves wondering how they can have victory in Christ

Chapter 1 Runaway Lover (Ingredient #1 Admitting Our Responsibility to Sin) This chapter highlights the key healing ingredient that we must step up to the bat and take responsibility for our sins and the way we have responded to the sin done to us. Using the key text of Genesis3:8 where Adam and Eve hid when confronted by God,

Chapter 2 That Old Dam (Ingredient #2 Placing Responsibility on Others for Their Sin Done to Us) This chapter zeroes in on John 8:32 and allows readers to not only know the truth, but also to do something with the truth in order to be set free. Because victims feel responsible for the sin done to them and often blame themselves for what happened, it is important for readers to redirect the blame of where it belongs...on their abuser. The chapter ends with a fictional metaphoric story entitle, That Old Dam allows readers the power and choice to truly be set free.

Chapter 3 The Lazarus Linens (Ingredient #3 Our Responsibility to Others) This chapter brings into focus the scripture where Jesus not only healed Lazarus from the dead, but also commanded others to take off Lazarus' grave clothes. It is the goal of this chapter to direct readers to realize that we all have a responsibility to others. We all have grave clothes, or things that prevent us from living the life God has called us to, and we are to help each other take off our grave clothes.

Chapter 4 Mirror Mirror on the Wall (Ingredient #4 Believing What is Fact Instead of What We Feel This chapter takes into account what all of us have done from time to time...believe what we feel instead of what is actually fact. Because we are only human, we will all struggle at some point in our lives with our feelings instead of what is actually true. When we are able to separate the two true healing begins to seep into our lives as medicine for our heartbroken souls.

Chapter 5 A Trip to the Dentist (Ingredient #5 Believing We Can Apply Medicine as Deep as the Wound Goes) Chapter five begins part two by looking at the reader's present state and the feelings that accompany our past wounds. Because we are emotional beings, we tend to dig up the past and focus on the triggers that keep us from living in the here and now.

Chapter 6 The Rain Gauge Renaissance (Ingredient #6 Believing We Can Stand Firmly in the Present One Day at a Time While Putting the Past into Proper Perspective) This chapter talks about Luke 21:19, *"By standing firm you will gain life." (NIV)* By looking at what is fact and not feelings, we can then move on to how to stand firm in the present. Readers will examine the good, the bad, and the ugly in their lives and be given the opportunity to rid themselves of anything that hinders them from living and standing firmly in today's world.

Chapter 7 The Promise of Satisfaction (Ingredient #7 Believing We Can be Satisfied in Today's World)This chapter takes a look at each reader's life and shows through scripture how she can be satisfied in today's world while at the same time yearning for the future. When we stop living in the past and are firmly girded in the present, we can then be content with what is happening in our lives today.

Chapter 8 The Promise of Peace (Ingredient #8 Believing We Can Have Peace on Earth) This chapter highlights the all elusive ingredient each of us is born with; a real need of peace in today's world. Because each of us is born into a fallen world, we lack the peace that only Christ can bring to our frail lives.

Chapter 9 A Pillar of Salt (Ingredient #9 Hoping for the Future When Our Past Keeps Coming Up) This chapter deals with the reality that each of us must face as believers; that many times our past keeps coming up no matter what the present or future says. The key text is Genesis 19 where Lot's wife turns into a pillar of salt because she looks back. Although we may not turn into a pillar of salt, Satan's certainly has a field day when we keep looking to the past instead of to the future.

Chapter 10 A Portrait of Hope (Ingredient #10 Hoping Against All Hope)The author uses the example of her close friend and prayer partner who underwent six months of chemotherapy while pregnant and gave birth to a 100% healthy daughter.

PART I

HEALING THE PAST

CHAPTER 1

Runaway Lover

Ingredient #1 Admitting Our Responsibility To Sin

Day 1
A Day to Confess

Psalm 32:5a "I will confess my transgressions to the Lord..." (NIV)

I had tried in vain for almost fifteen years to stop. Sure, I'd had some success with spurts of sobriety for months at a time. However, my secret was getting harder and harder to contain. It seemed to insidiously seep into other areas of my life. It affected my physical health, my emotional health, as well as my spiritual health. It's not like I didn't pray about it. I asked, no, begged God to help me quit. Finally I had decided to cease going to Him out of fear of abandonment. Why couldn't I win this particular battle in my life. I had asked God that a million times. Then suddenly, a friend's word illuminated the problem. How can you have victory over one particular shameful area when you haven't dealt with all the other shameful events in your life?

I had reasoned for over a decade that my struggle with laxatives was not my fault. I contemplated that it was a result of having been wounded, or hurt, in my life. So what if I had one particularly shameful secret? It was because of what was done to me. Then, as if a spotlight had been directed on me, I awoke one morning lamenting the progress of my life. Simply put, I hated it. I hated every vile inch of my life. Moreover, I loathed myself.

It's been years since then, but along the way I have discovered 10 ingredients to healing a wounded life. There is one basic premise I want to focus on during this bible study. Why can't we win or heal if we are Christians? After all, haven't we got the ultimate answer? His name is Jesus. I want to use Jeremiah 8:22 to reference why so many millions are believers face a lack of emotional healing.

"Is there no balm in Gilead? Is there no physician there? Why then is there no healing for the wound of my people?" (Jeremiah 8:22, NIV

Friend, thanks for coming with me on this intimate journey as we face the question to why we cannot, or do not, heal as wounded believers. I wish I could tell you that my struggle with laxatives is over but it isn't. I wish I could tell you I don't crave them, but I do. What I can do in response to this is to get up and face it one day at a time. I can't worry about tomorrow. I only have the strength to face today.

Jeremiah, the Old Testament prophet, hits on a key nerve in the Christian community then and today. Basically, he is asking why can we not heal if we have the key ingredient, Jesus?

Record Jeremiah 46:11 here.

Record Jeremiah 51:8 here.

Gilead was the mecca of healing according to scripture. Jeremiah tells the people that Gilead's balm is healing, unlike their vain attempts to heal themselves. Will we as Christians have pain? Most assuredly we will. We will all need the balm that Gilead offers.

Jeremiah raises a key, if not the key, question for hurting believers. If there is balm, or healing ingredients in Gilead, then why are we not healed?

How can God not heal our past?

Is not Jesus the balm we need?

I had Christ, but remained unhealed with my laxative use. Along my recovery way, I discovered twelve ingredients that I believe to be the balm of Jesus. Won't you join me on this intimate road to recovery? Again, I am not an expert. My evidence is simple. My theory personal. My pain real. I have lived a wounded life and have yearned for healing like nothing else. Come with me as we discover key ingredients that make the balm healing medicine for our tattered lives.

Let me be clear. While you may insist that some grave sin was done to you, I will address that in chapter two. For now, let's take an honest look on the inside. Yes, your struggle area may be a direct result of having been wounded. Perhaps you too have an eating disorder, or maybe it is an alcohol problem, codependency, lying, drugs, or whatever the result of your shame As insane as this may sound, I personally justified my laxative use because of the wounds or hurts that had culminated in my life. One shameful event entailed another shameful addiction. I agree with John

Bradshaw when he says that all addictions are the result of shame. *(Healing the Shame that Binds You)* I told myself many lies as to why I needed the laxatives. If you are anything like me, you probably have minimized your addiction or wound. Perhaps you justify it too. But when the lights are out and the night crawls in bed with you, don't you have the sinking feeling of hiding? Only there is nothing more naked than our sin. This is a fact that goes all the way back to the beginning of time.

What is your area of wound?

How have you responded to this hurt?

Have you struggled with any particular sin area in your life as a result of having been wounded?

Record the following verses on confessing our sin:

1 John 1:9

Psalm 38:18

Daniel 9:20-23

What was Daniel given as a result of having confessed his sin and the sin of his people?

If we confess our sin, God is sure to forgive us totally. Scripture is also very clear that we gain wisdom and insight as a result of going to Him humbly admitting our responsibility to sin. Confessing cleanses our soul and spirit. We have everything to gain and nothing to lose. Let's do that today. We'll be glad we did.

Day 2
A Day to Hide

Genesis 3:8 "Then the man and his wife heard the sound of the Lord God as he was walking in garden in the cool of the day, and they hid..." (NIV)

It's genetic. It's in our family tree. It was passed down to us. Don't feel bad about it. Just acknowledge it and accept it. Like I said earlier, it goes back to the beginning of time. Let's venture back there shall we?

Adam and Eve were created in a perfect state of being and lived in a perfect place. The Garden of Eden. They lacked nothing. They walked and talked with God on a daily basis. Then, out of nowhere, Satan deceives Eve and she gives in and eats the forbidden fruit.

Record what Genesis 3:6 says.

How does scripture describe the fruit?

Do you find that sin is desirable at some point before you proceed to sin?

Did Eve think eating the fruit would help her gain wisdom?

Could that have been another reason she ate the fruit?

The first taste of shame, resulting from sin, is introduced in The Garden. "Then the eyes of both of them were opened, and they realized they were naked; so they sewed fig leaves together and made coverings for themselves." (Genesis 3:7, NIV)Look at what happens next. God was walking in The Garden of Eden and couldn't find Adam and Eve. Of course, realize that God really knew where they were, but asks them anyway.

What were Adam and Eve doing? (Genesis 3:8)

They were hiding from Him. "…and they hid from the Lord God among the trees of the garden." (Genesis 3:8, NIV)

What was the immediate action Adam and Eve took when they sinned?

Why did they do this you think?

Whenever we sin, our first line of defense is to hide from God. We can thank Adam and Eve for that. One reason that they hid from God in The Garden was due to their shame. Before they sinned and ate of the fruit, they had no shame. Look at what Genesis 2:25 says. "The man and his wife were both naked, and they felt no shame.(NIV) Adam and Eve had been created in utter perfection. There was no shame in being naked before each other and before God. However, when Satan came into the picture everything went out the door. Eve mistakenly thought God was holding out on her. She thought God wasn't being quite honest with her. Satan tricks her into thinking that:

She can be like God if she eats the fruit

She will not die spiritually if she eats the fruit

She will gain wisdom if she eats the fruit

So, what does Eve do? Of course she eats the fruit. And the end result? Shame. Pure and simple. "Then the eyes of both of them were opened, and they realized they were naked; so they sewed fig leaves together and made coverings for themselves." (Genesis 3:6 NIV)The reason Adam and Eve hid from God in The Garden was because of their shame. Sin causes shame. As a result of having been wounded in my life, I turned to laxatives to try and rid myself of my shame. Did this help matters? Of course not. It only made my shame worse. In taking the laxatives for fifteen years, I was trapped in a cycle of sin and shame. Round and round it went. How was I to get off the merry-go round? I had to finally take a cold hard look at myself and say "although I was hurt in very real ways, I responded by sinning. Did the shame stop instantly? No. I won't lie to you. It took a lot of hard work, pain, and a new day each day to convince myself that I could live life without the shame and sin of laxative use. Does the shame ever go away? I'm glad to tell you it does. Not overnight, but through declarations of God's amazing grace. But it all starts with ingredient #1; Admitting our responsibility to sin. It's not easy when we have addictions due to sin and shame. What must we do in order to admit our sin?

First we must be humble. It takes a humble heart to admit our wrong doings. Next, we must be honest. Remember the woman who bled for twelve years who touched the edge of Jesus' cloak? Notice in scripture what she did when Jesus called her forth. She fell at his feet (humility) and told *"the whole truth." (Mark 5:33b, NIV)* If we are to ever be healed by Jesus of our wounds, we must be willing to tell Him the entire truth, not just some or most of it. The whole truth. And it starts with confessing our sin to God. Why not make today the day of confession? Let's make today a day of healing.

Day 3
A Day to Blame

*Genesis 3:12 "The woman **you** put here with me-she gave me some fruit from the tree, and I ate it." (NIV)*

I hear it every day. Well, almost every day. As a teacher in the public school system, I am accustomed to hearing just about anything. "Johnny, stop talking." "Well, Cindy Lou took my pencil and I was just asking for it back." Or better yet, "Mary was about to hit me so I went ahead and hit her." If you can imagine it, a school child will do it. They pull no punches. What you see is what you get. Never once have I called on a kid where they lower their head and confess their sin. What is their natural reaction to being called upon for their error-way-infraction? They blame it on another person. This happens in my classroom without fail. But you know what? It's hereditary I'm afraid.

Let's take another peek at Adam and Eve in The Garden.

First, we know that Adam and Eve hid from God because of their shame. They were afraid of God after they sinned.

Record Genesis 3:8-10 here.

Notice carefully, did Adam and Eve lie to God?

First Adam and Eve *justify* the sin of disobeying God. They don't exactly lie, they justify their actions *through* the defense mechanism of *blaming* another person. We all do it. It goes back to The Garden of Eden. When God directly confronts Adam, Adam then justifies his actions by blaming God Himself.

How does Adam do this?

Adam blames God because it was God who gave Adam the woman. Again, look at Genesis 3:12. In other words, Adam says something along these lines…"Look God, it isn't my fault. That woman that you gave me made me do it. It wasn't my idea, it was hers. Remember God, you gave her to me. If you hadn't given her to me this would be a mute issue.

What happens next? Look at Genesis 3:13.

Instead of owning up to her sin, Eve then blames Satan. Notice again that she doesn't lie exactly. She merely justifies her sin to God by placing the blame on the serpent. Thus, it is in our genetic makeup to justify our original sin by placing the blame on another person. I did this for almost two decades. "Well, you see God, I take the laxatives because of the wounds by another person. There is so much shame that I must use the laxatives to try and hide. It's not that bad. I do it to control my weight. So it is not my fault really. It is another person's fault and actions that gives me no choice but to take the laxatives." Or something to that effect. I blamed others for my control issue with laxatives.

Have you ever blamed another person for your own sin issue or issues?

Did it bring healing or freedom?

What was the outcome of doing that?

Isn't it comforting friend that we are not alone in our struggle to be healed. What is our first response when we sin? We turn or hide or runaway from God. I did this for over a decade. Somewhere in my mind I would think that if I hid or ran away from God that He would, for some reason, not be as mad at me if I waited a while before going to Him Can you relate? Please share with the group if you feel comfortable

What's our next line of defense? We pass the buck. It's not our fault we sinned. We even blame God like Adam did. First we hide, then we blame. What if I told you ingredient #1 is to accept responsibility for our sin. I cannot tell you the freedom it brings when we finally accept responsibility for our sin and stop blaming others. When we do this we open the windows of healing and close the door of shame and sin. When we stop hiding and making excuses we open up God's hand to heal us. Confessing is good for the soul. It brings balm into our wounded lives.

Day 4
A Day of Clothing

Genesis 3:21 "The Lord God made garments of skin for Adam and his wife and clothed them." (NIV)

What was God's response to Adam and Eve sinning? Look up Genesis 3:14-20

Yes, there were consequences to their sin. We can't really be realistic and think that there would be no consequences to their disobedience. Sometimes I think we are afraid to go to God and confess because we mistakenly think His consequences are punishments. That's not true at all.

Describe the difference between consequence versus punishment.

What were the consequences for Eve's disobedience? Look up Genesis 3:16.

What were the consequences for Adam's disobedience? Look up Genesis 3:17-19.

Do you think God was mad at Adam and Eve for their disobedience? Why or why not?

What was God's response to Adam and Eve's sin? First He tells them the consequences to their sin. Then watch the next thing God does. Remember it. Engrave it on your mind God then loves them. What Debbie? Are you sure? How do you know this? Watch the compassion of God at work.

"The Lord God made garments of skin for Adam and his wife and clothed them." *(Genesis 3:21, NIV)* Even in Adam and Eve's sin and shame, God lovingly makes Garments of skin and clothed them. God wasn't mad. He didn't say, "I'm sick of your excuses. I'm sick of your same old sins." No, God compassionately provided a parallel example of the most loving event of all time…the cross. A sacrifice of an animal was necessary for Adam and Eve in order to be clothed. They didn't clothe themselves. Well, actually they did. But it never compared to God's clothing. A fig leaf versus a fur coat leaves a lot to be desired. If God didn't love them so much He would have left them in their sin and shame, but He didn't. And the same is true for us today.

Describe the difference between Adam and Eve clothing themselves compared to God clothing them?

In what ways do you try to 'clothe yourself?'

Friend, isn't it time we traded a fig leaf for a fur coat? Instead of hiding and passing the buck, why not get out of the shame of whatever your wound is and accept God's clothing, or healing. Don't keep dodging responsibility to your sin. Own up to it. Tell God you've made fig leaves and want that fur coat.

When I finally admitted to a friend about my laxative use and owned up to it, the healing balm of Gilead came pouring over me. No more lies. No more secrets. The physician is in Gilead. His name is Jesus. Sure, we genetically run from God and blame others. So what. All of us do it. Won't you be the one to admit your sin and open up the healing for God to come into your life and make a covering for you? Don't be a runaway lover. Let your love, Christ, apply the medicine to heal you. Own up to your sins. This is ingredient #1. Let's allow this balm to enter our hearts and souls and bring healing today.

Day 5
A Day of Truth

John 8:32 "Then you will know the truth and the truth will set you free."
(NIV)

Bondage. Chains. Prisoner. I've been there friend. I bet you have too. I longed for the liberation from my chains of sin and shame. But it didn't come. For years I moaned and groaned as to why I was stuck in the muck and mire of my addictions. I yelled at God. I cursed at God. I even gave God the middle finger. Literally. Still, freedom was only a dream.

What keeps us from being free from our sin and shame?

What have you done to escape the chains of your hurts and wounds?

I believe there are several things that keep us from experience the healing balm of Christ. First of all, let's take a look at a well known verse, John 8:32. *"Then you will know the truth and the truth will set you free."* (NIV) At first glance we may think this verse is easy as pie. If I just know the truth I will be free. Let me assure you of this…it is a little more involved than that. What? I thought if you merely knew the truth you would be set free. Isn't that what God's Word says? Not exactly.

If you study the Greek language in this verse, John 8:32, the word, *to know*, literally means to know as in the consummation of marriage. To know means to know intimately. That is, you must *do* something with the truth. When a husband and wife know each other intimately, they act upon that truth. That is what the word, to know, in this verse means. We must take action with the truth. I must do more than to know or to acknowledge that I am an alcoholic. I must take action to that effect.

Why do you think this verse uses the Greek language to communicate its meaning?

What steps or actions have you taken to be healed from your wounds?

Record here what 2 Timothy 2:9 says.

One reason I believe we don't heal is that we don't take steps with the truth and also believe we don't let God's Word bring freedom. In 2Timothy 2:9 it says that *God word is not chained." (NIV)* Can God's Word bring freedom and healing? Quite simply, yes it can.

Look up and record the following verses on the Word of God.

Philippians 2:16

2 Samuel 22:31

Psalm 119:105

Proverbs 30:5

James 1:22

John 17:17a

God's Word can bring healing and freedom *if* we know the truth of it and *do* something with that truth. We can't just merely glance its' way. We must study it pray about it, and put God's Word into action. Then, the healing balm of the truth of God's Word can come pouring into our lives. This is indeed what sets us free.

Once again, it is interesting to note the case with the woman who bled for twelve years. This woman had the faith to believe that if she just merely touched the edge of Jesus' cloak, she would be healed. However, notice that after she did this Jesus asked the crowd who had touched him. (Mark 5:27-31) Of course, Jesus already knew who had touched him. But, Jesus wanted the woman to know for sure she was healed.

Jesus didn't want this woman to merely feel she was healed, He wanted her to know without a doubt she was indeed healed.

What does Mark 5:33 say she did?

Note that the woman who bled for twelve years does two things. First of all, she falls at Jesus' feet. She is humble and knows she is in the presence of greatness. When we go to God, are we acting in true humility? After all, He is the creator of the universe. Next, she tells Jesus the "whole truth." Not some or almost all of it. No, she tells Him the entire truth.

Record what Mark 5:34 says.

Jesus tells this woman, or daughter, as He affectionately and lovingly calls her, that her faith has healed her and she is to go in peace and be freed from her suffering. Friend, that can be a picture of us and what God desires to do with our wounds. We must have the faith that God can and does truly desire to heal us from our wounds or hurts. However, we must be willing to tell Him the entire truth and to do something with that truth. We must do what the Greek prompts us to do...to know the truth intimately, as in the consummation of marriage. Are we willing to take steps of action with the truth of our sin and shame? Let's don't be a runaway lover who runs or hides from God when facing our sin. Let's don't blame others for our own actions. Let's step up to the bat of responsibility and admit or confess our sin to God. Then let's do something with that truth. It is only then that the healing balm of Jesus will flow graciously into our lives and repair the damage done to us over the years. This is ingredient #1 and the first step we must be willing to take if we are to experience God's true healing for our lives. Don't delay. Act today. You'll be glad you did. We have nothing to lose and everything to gain.

Prayer: Dear Lord, thank you that you are a compassionate God. We never have to fear coming to you. Help us not to hide or run away from you because of fear. Help us to come boldly to you in our time of need and to confess our sin to you. Help us not to blame others for our wrongs in life. Clothe us in your coverings and give us the strength to not try and clothe ourselves when we sin. Apply the healing balm to our lives that comes from admitting our responsibility to sin. We know that we must do something with our truths and not merely acknowledge them. Thank you that you allow us to come at any time and for any reason into your presence. Give us the courage to come today. We pray these things in your name, Amen.

Write out your prayer below in the space provide below

CHAPTER 2

That Old Dam

Ingredient #2 Placing Responsibility on Others for Their Sin Done to Us

Day 1
The Power of Weakness

2 Corinthians 12:9 "My grace is sufficient for you, for my power is made perfect in weakness." (NIV)

Perhaps you unknowingly push it back into the dark recesses of your mind. Maybe you catch yourself thinking about it from time to time. Or, if you are like me, it has manifested itself in an addiction. "It" is the emotional, physical, or spiritual pain that has thrust itself into your life and has yet to vacate. I thought for many years that the wounds in my life were my fault. I responded with self-hatred. The predominate emotion I felt was shame. I sensed that something was wickedly wrong with myself. As children of pain we cannot decipher between something that was done to us as wrong versus something that is wrong with ourselves. Sin and shame go down to the core of our being. Where there is sin, shame is not far behind.

Do you currently feel any shame in your life for anything that has happened to you?

How have you responded to that shame?

Shame attaches itself in addictions in our lives as Bradshaw shows in his classic book, *Healing the Shame that Binds You.* Are we or are we not responsible for the reaction to the sin done to us? We are not responsible for the emotional scars done to us.

However, we are responsible for our sinful response to that sin. It is worth noting that addictions are the natural progressions when shame is involved in the process. It is what it is.

King David was the most powerful man in Israel. He had a heart that loved God. We know he loved God dearly because of the Psalms. But, as all of us are, he was human. He strayed from God, like all of us do from time to time. He committed adultery with Bathsheba. An affair to remember for sure. He murdered Uriah, her husband. All these things were done after he was a believer and not before. Sometimes I think we have a mentality that we should not sin greatly as a believer. Sure, we can sin the small sins, but what about the big sins. We listen to testimonials by people who say that their struggle with sin and shame are over with. As inspiring as some testimonials may be, I believe these people are doing a disservice to the millions and millions of Christians who struggle on a daily, or weekly basis with whatever sins or addictions they may have because if the sin done to them.

Have you ever heard a testimonial by someone who inspired you?

What was it about their story that motivated you?

We, as Christians, are not perfect. To believe we will not sin is outlandish. How are we to change? Do we shame someone to change in the church? Many times I think we do. But Jesus never shamed anyone to change. Jesus, the only perfect person to walk the earth, had a different way. He compassionately took someone and loved them to change in His timing, not the church's timing.

One fear I had was the ability to change. I was a victim stuck in the shame of my addiction. While we must not take responsibility for the sin done to us, we must think in terms of a survivor's mentality and not a victim's mentality. We can change, with the help of God, not because we are superior Christians, but because in our own humanness or weakness Christ is revealed.

Look up and record 2 Corinthians 12:9

What do you think Paul means by this verse?

Paul, God's ambassador in chains, knew weakness. He was stoned, beaten, and put in prison for doing God's will and work. I don't know if you have ever been in jail, but I have. For a year I went every Friday night to our local jail through Prison Fellowship Ministry and shared the Word of God with the female inmates. Just to let you know, I didn't have a lot of power or choices. Never had I felt so weak or helpless. But then something amazing happened to me. I never felt so much at home before. The power of God reigned supreme and I knew for the first time in my life what the power of weakness was all about. When we, as believers, give our will over to God in stressful and difficult circumstances, we are empowered by His strength and not ours.

Look up the following verses on weakness:

2 Timothy 1:16

Colossians 4:18

Ephesians 6:20

Romans 9:17

2 Corinthians 13:4

Go ahead and give God your weakness. There is power in it. I can't really explain it. but there is. He wants nothing more than to soothe our hurts and pains with His healing balm. Think your weakness is shameful? It isn't. It's only human. And God delights in humans. It's all He's got to work with. Will He restore us? Yes, just ask David and Bathsheba. What He did for them He can do for us today.

Day 2
The Power of Action

2 Corinthians 9:2b "…has stirred most of them to action." (NIV)

For years and years I lamented my bulimia. I cried. No, I wailed and wailed to be healed. I prayed about it. I fasted. I did everything known to mankind. Then, one day on a five mile run, it dawned on me. I was doing everything except acting upon it. My plan needed action.

Do you think as believers we pray more than we act upon something?

Is it Biblical to act and then pray or is the reverse true to you?

I sometimes think we as Christians are afraid to go all out and act upon something, as if it is not being spiritual. How badly we want to be healed by God depends a large part if we are *willing* to do whatever it takes to be healed. Do we have enough humility to act upon a plan set to action? God will never heal us if we are not willing to go the distance with Him. Take the paralytic for example. Let's look at that picture of healing in scripture.

Record what Mark 2:1-5 says.

It's no secret that Jesus by this time was widely popular. He was in Capernaum, probably at Peter's home. A large crowd had gathered and there was hardly any room for people to listen to Him. Notice scripture says, "…not even outside the door." (Mark 2:2b, NIV) Thus, there was basically no room inside nor outside the house for people to hear Jesus' words.

Record Mark 2:3

All it says is that four men came bringing a paralytic to Jesus. We assume that the four men were either friends or relatives of the paralytic. We know they cared about the paralytic, because they carried him to Jesus, the miracle worker. When they went to Jesus at the home, they could not get in. What were they to do?

What would you have done if you were one of the four friends carrying the paralytic and you couldn't have gotten to Jesus? Would you have turned around and went home?

But not these four men. All we know is that they, not to mention the paralytic, were desperate. "Since they could not get to Jesus because of the crowd, they made an opening in the roof above Jesus and, after digging through it, lowered the mat the paralyzed man was lying on." (Mark 2:4, NIV)

How do we know they were desperate?

Did you see it? They actually *dug* through the roof with their hands. Now, that's what I call desperate. I use to have this image in my mind how they went on the roof and just lowered their friend into Jesus' presence. But that is not accurate. First of all, they had to climb on the roof and then hoist up their paralyzed friend *and* the mat. But let's not stop there. Next, they had to dig through the roof with their bare hands. That's not an easy task. They took no tools for doing this with them. Remember, they went to get healing, not bringing their hammers or tools to break through a tough straw roof.

Are you desperate enough in your own healing to "dig through a roof?"

What are you doing today to accomplish that means?

But the story doesn't stop there. After they lower the paralytic to Jesus, Jesus says what?

Mark 2:5?

Scripture says that "when Jesus saw their *faith...*" (Mark 2:5, NIV) Faith requires action sometimes. Faith is not idle. Jesus desires for us to act upon that faith. What if the four men had gone home? But they wanted their friend to be healed, so much as to dig with bare hands through a roof they had labored to climb upon. Yes, if we are to experience true healing we must be willing to go the distance with Christ. Is it easy? No, it may require a lot of hard sweat and tears. It may be difficult. It may cost us. But rest assured, it will be worth it.

I hate to repeat myself, but let's be reminded again of what the Greek word for "to know" means in John 8:32. We must know the truth in order to be set free. It is not merely an intellectual knowing, but rather to know means to know as in the consummation of marriage. That is, we must act in order for us to be set free. A marriage is not a marriage until the intimate act of consummation takes place. That involves action, not mere knowledge.

Are you knowing the truth as in acting it out?

What is keeping you from being healed in your opinion?

Friend, let's not just pray about something like healing, let's put it into action. Let's work hard to bring it to fruition. If four men can bring their paralyzed friend to Jesus and dig through a roof for his healing, let's do the same. Our faith must bring with it action. The balm is in Gilead, and His name is Jesus. Let's just make sure we are willing to do our part in order to be healed.

Day 3
The Power of Love

2 Timothy 1:7 "For God did not give us a spirit of timidity, but a spirit of power, of love…" (NIV)

It has been said that love is the most powerful force in the universe. I couldn't agree more. After all, haven't we all done some pretty interesting things all in the name of love? I know I have. Not all of them have been smart moves either. I can remember one time being in the fifth grade and eating a whole box of thin mints just to be able to sit at the school cafeteria a little longer to be near Randy McKinney. My mind told me to sit there and munch and munch while my stomach begged me to stop. What did my heart say? Well, it told me that Randy loved me. The truth of the matter was that he loved my cookies so he sat beside me. I was convinced it was love. True love. Later, after some time had passed, I vividly recall barfing my guts up. No Randy. No love. I still get sick on thin mints to this day.

Do you think there is power in love?

Have you ever done something you later regretted all in the name of love?

How did it make you feel?

I'm a hopeless romantic. Give me a movie with a guy and girl who fall in love and live happily ever after...and some popcorn and a pickle...and I'm content. I believe love is what ultimately guides us. Even in our worst moments, the times we had rather forget, I still believe love is at the root of our actions. Whether it is love for a thing, such as money, or love of self, it is still love. What gets me is that sometimes we are motivated not by the love of God, or others, but the carnal love of the world. Still, in its' most basic fundamentals, it is love.

Let's take a look at someone who was motivated by the love of Christ, the most prolific love there is. This person devoted herself to what I call the ultimate love of all time...the love of Jesus. Her name? Mary of Bethany. You know the story. She had a sister named hurry-up-and-help-me, or Martha. She also had a dead-man-walketh- brother named Lazarus.

Read and record John 12:1-8.

What does John 12:1-2 say was going on?

Who was the dinner in honor of?

Describe what you believe was taking place at this dinner.

Record what John 12:3 says.

Scripture says that Mary took an expensive perfume and poured it on Jesus' feet and wiped his feet with her hair. Did you see it? Mary took something that cost a lot, in this case, the perfume, and sacrificially gave it to Christ. Whenever we give from our hearts the cost is dear. Perhaps we don't give God things that financially cost a lot, but there are other ways in which we give things to Him that are near and dear to us.

Can you list some of the 'things' that you have given over to God that mean a lot to you?

We can give God things that mean a lot to us that are emotional, spiritual, and physical. I don't think it is an accident that God's Word says that Mary took an expensive perfume, nard, and poured it over Jesus. The meaning here is both literal as well as figurative.

Can you remember a time when you gave someone something that meant a great deal to you?

How did it make you feel when you gave it to that person?

What was your main motivation in giving that person something that meant so much to you?

Look at John 12:3b. What is the next thing Mary does?

Notice that Mary then wiped Jesus' feet and wiped them with her hair. Why is this in Scripture?

I believe it is in God's perfect Word because her love was so intense *and* spontaneous. If her actions had been thought through and planned then she wouldn't have used her hair as an instrument to wipe Jesus' feet. She would have brought or gotten a towel from the kitchen. Have you ever noticed that sometimes love is so immense that we just instantly do something, not thinking out the plans? I believe this was the case with Mary. Her hair serves as a constant reminder that she was *desperate* to communicate her love for her Savior.

What is the most desperate thing you have ever done for love?

Again, what were you trying to communicate in your most desperate act?

Notice what happens when we love from our hearts. Don't miss this important verse.

"And the house was filled with the fragrance of the perfume."

Whenever we love from a pureness of our souls, there is a miracle that takes place. It is called sacrifice. What Mary did that day in her home was pure sacrifice. She gave from her heart to communicate to her Lord love. Unabandoned love. And guess what the outcome was? A sweet aroma that filled the entire house. Love has a funny way of doing that. God knows without a doubt when we give to Him or someone out of our love for Him. It is a sacrifice born out of love. Sound familiar? It's what Christ is all about. His love for us. How do we know this? Because of the sacrifice He became for us. Why? Because He loves us.

What does 2 Corinthians 2:15 say we are?

Why do you think God's Word says *"and the house was filled?"*

    Love, the power of love has an amazing effect on us humans. It fills up the emptiness of our souls. The pain. The loneliness. The addictions. The abuse. The dysfunction. It soothes the soul like nothing else. After all, God is love, and until we come to Him we are in constant search of what, or who, can fill us up. I believe that is the power of love. That's the power of Christ. That's why we are all vegabonds of deep who wander this earth in search of what only our Creator can fill. And when we find it we will want to give it to others to communicate to them what was given to us on that fateful Friday: the power of love.

Day 4
The Power of Miracles

1 Corinthians 6:14 "By his power God raised the Lord from the dead..."
(NIV)

Have you ever been sure of a miracle in your life?

What happened? Please share with the group if you feel comfortable.

Why do you think miracles happen?

What would you tell someone who did not believe in miracles?

Look up the following verses on miracles:

Galatians 3:5

2 Corinthians 12:12

Psalm 77:11

John 10:25

Look up Philippians 3:20-21 and record.

Why do you think God allows suffering in this world?

Look up the following verses on suffering and record:

Romans 5:3

Romans 8:17-18

Philippians 3:10

1 Peter 4:13

1 Peter 5:9

What kind of emotions do you think the women at the cross felt?

Have you ever witnessed something so addictive and yet terrible at the same time?

How did it make you feel?

Please share with the group if you feel comfortable.

Isn't that just like God? To bring us to such a strange place to witness His miracles? There is power in miracles. The power to change lives. No matter what has happened in our lives, God *can* bring healing. No matter our issues, dysfunction, sins, hurts, and on and on it goes. Even if the sin done to us is not our fault, we must place responsibility on the person or persons who did it to us and not God or ourselves. That, in and of itself, is a miracle. And miracles take courage. Rarely does a miracle take place without the courage of the one who participates in it. Mary had to have courage to believe and act upon the miracle of being told she was pregnant by the Holy Spirit. Mary and Martha had to have the courage to believe that Jesus could raise their brother from the grave. Rahab had to have the courage to hide the spies in her home and believe she and her family would be spared from death. And you and I must have the courage to believe in the power of the miracle of God healing us from past wounds. Today, if you suffer the effects of blaming yourself or God for some hurt done to you, please let yourself off the hook and place responsibility on the person responsible for it. I'm not saying to not forgive, but merely to take a hard look at what happened. It takes a miracle to change, but there is power in that miracle. I sure am not where I want to be, but thank God I'm not where I use to be. We can change and heal. This is the power of miracles.

Day 5
The Power of God

1 Peter 1:3 "His divine power has given us everything we need for life..." (NIV)

Sometimes the more things change the more they stay the same.

Have you ever felt this way?

What do you think this saying means?

Do you believe the verse above is true? Why or why not?

What is the biggest barrier to having victory in our lives and healing?

Have you ever felt like it was impossible to change?

Look up and record the following verses:

Ephesians 1:19

1 Corinthians 1:25

Because God has divinely given us His power in our lives we *do* have the power to change and heal. However, many times it doesn't just fall from the sky. We must many times implement the power of God into our lives through action, hard work, and change. Even if those around us never think we will change. Let me tell you a story that illustrates this theory of mine. It's about an old man who nobody thought would ever change.

That Old Dam

After years and years the old dam broke. Many of the townspeople were stunned; their lives held captive by the overflow of water. Everyone was caught off guard. Except for Red.

Red was the little old man who fished every day at that old dam. Whether it was 100 degrees in August and he had to battle the stifling summer heat with no hint of a hot breeze, or it was a snowing day in December, his frozen fingers wrapped around his old cane pole, Red went fishing just the same.

One day a town committee went to Red's home to ask him questions about that old dam.

"Did you see it coming?"

"Did you know ahead of time? Is that why you stopped fishing?"

"We know you didn't know, otherwise you would have let the town folks know."

Red let them answer their own questions more or less, and he chuckled with his tongue in cheek. "Yes," he thought to himself. He'd seen it coming. He knew the dam would one day break. But he never knew exactly when.

Red didn't just merely watch the red and white plastic cork bob up and down. He'd look around every now and then while fishing on that old dam. That dam he'd fished on for over sixty-five years.

The cracks in that old dam slowly evolved into larger ones. Day after day. Month after month. Year after year.

Red had grown to love that old dam, accustomed not to the fishing, for he never caught many fish, but rather he'd grown to love the solitude and peace that the sound the water brought. The consistent ebb of its blue.

But one day the sound of the water began to change.

Yes, an architect could have inspected that old dam as the town committee had thought about-after the dam gave way.

It almost killed him that day. Not when the dam actually broke, but when he made the decision to stop going to that old dam.

There was something safe about that familiar place. That familiar sight. That familiar smell. His familiar spot on that old dam.

Red knew he didn't have a choice, but then again he did. Stay and be swept away, or leave and mourn that old dam a little sooner.

The people in town just knew Red would die an old old man fishing on that old dam. But they were wrong. It all changed for Red when the peculiarness of the water became predictable. It just wasn't the same for him on that old dam. He began to question the safety in the familiar.

If he left the dam and his spot, he'd have to find something else to do with his time. That frightened Red. In fact, he almost chose to stay on the dam and be swept away.

But then one day Red did it. He left that old dam, his place marking the exact spot where the dam would later break.

It almost did kill him, leaving that old dam. But one day when the air was cool and light, the smell of the freshly cut lawn was sweet, and an easiness in the day was felt, Red began to see something that that old dam did not offer him. A chance to live. To experience new things. New sounds. New sights. His spot changed the day he left that old dam.

It never ceased to amaze Red when he was out and about in his new life how many people said it must be killing him to not be fishing at the dam.

But Red would always answer this question by putting his weathered hands deep within his pockets, poking around his sparse spare change, and while the old dam breaking was reaking havoc on the town, Red would think to himself, the foreboding flood allowed him the chance of a lifetime. That which he thought would kill him actually saved his life.

And so it was o.k. when the townspeople laid old Red to rest in the cemetery under the blooming Bradford pear.

They thought old Red had died of a broken heart. Oh, if they only knew the truth about his heart…giving out because of the fullness of life he was living.

But it was o.k. with Red; because he knew the truth about that old dam. (Debbie Vanderslice, *Shameless,* New Hope Publishers, 2008)

What is 'your old dam?' Please share with the group if you feel comfortable.

What do you need in order to have the power to change your circumstances?

Is fear one of the factors keeping you from healing?

I believe if we want to live a victorious life and experience healing one day at a time we must stop blaming ourselves for sin done to us. Yes, we may have responded to the abuse done to us in a sinful way but we are only human. Let's stop blaming ourselves and start healing by placing responsibility on others who have harmed us instead of beating up ourselves and God. He will provide everything we need in order to heal. So whether you are like me and have been drowning in a sea of self blame, stop and consider God's amazing power. He will provide everything we need. The first step is always the hardest and most frightening. But He'll walk through it with us one day at a time. We can change. We can heal as we go through this healing process one day at a time.

Prayer: Surround us with positive, caring, and support people who will spur us on to experience the balm in Gilead. Give us the courage to take action, love, and change into our broken lives. We know with your help we can become all you want us to become. In Jesus' name. Amen.

Prayer: Thank you God for molding us in your image. Help us stay on track and seeking you.

Write out your own prayer to God in the space provided below.

CHAPTER 3

The Lazarus Linens

Ingredient #3 Our Responsibility to Others

Day 1
Linens of Waiting

John 11:6 "Yet when he heard that Lazarus was sick, he stayed where he was two more days." (NIV)

We've all heard the story in Scripture about Lazarus and Jesus raising him from the dead. It's a miraculous story about the healing power of Christ. Is there anything we can learn from it and apply it to our lives for our own healing? I think there is.

Do you believe we have a responsibility to others? Why or why not?

In our own recovery and healing why is it important to be careful when helping others. Can helping others become unhealthy for us in some manner or why? Please explain. When we help others it can be a double edge sword. On one hand we are helping someone who really needs assistance. On the other hand, it can be a form of sickness if we continue to rescue that person when he or she could help themselves. I think that form of helping is called codependency. Have you been there friend?

Have you ever been codependent on someone?

How has that impacted your life?

When Jesus commanded others to help Lazarus take off his grave clothes, it wasn't a form of codependency. It was the purest form of Christian service in helping Lazarus get on with his life and discard the clothes, or issues if you will, that kept him from being all he could be. Lazarus couldn't do it on his own. He needed his brothers and sisters to help him. But notice an important detail in this miraculous story. Jesus *waited* a couple of days before going to Lazarus' hometown. Many scholars say Jesus did this for the sole purpose of letting everyone, mainly the religious leaders, know that Lazarus was truly and without a doubt dead as doornails. However, I think there was another reason.

I believe Jesus waited because He wanted the time to be right to heal Lazarus. Right as in the timing for others, such as Lazarus' sisters, to witness the others taking off Lazarus' grave clothes. Maybe Jesus was ministering to others that day as well and not merely the family of Lazarus.

Do you have grave clothes or things that prevent you from living the life God has called you to live?

What are you doing to get rid of those grave linens?

Waiting is such a key element in this story of Christ. Sometimes God allows us to wallow around in muck and mire until we are ready to be healed.

Look up the following verses on waiting and record:

Hebrews 9:28

Psalm 130:5-6

Isaiah 30:18

Romans 8:23

Titus 2:13

There seems to be a consistent theme in the Bible regarding waiting. Sometimes it is God's will for us to wait for Him and His timing. I think this can also refer to His healing us. He waited before going to raise Lazarus from the dead. He didn't just arrive on the scene and snap His finger. No, Jesus wept. (John 11:35) He *waited* before speaking His words of healing.

Why do you think Jesus waited (and wept) before raising Lazarus from the dead?

Have there been things you have had to wait for in your life a long time?

What impact has this waiting had on your life?

Many times I have had to wait in my yucky old linens while waiting to be healed. That hasn't occurred overnight. Maybe you have had to wait for a child for many years. Or maybe it is a marriage that won't heal. A relationship that continually gets worse each year. An addiction or two. A self-loathing perhaps. Whatever your grave clothes are, taking heart. God doesn't expect us to wait forever. He is merely waiting until we are ready to be healed from our grave clothes. I call it our linens of waiting. The time will come when we are ready. Ready to be healed. We must be active participants in our road to healing. We cannot just stand idly by and expect God to do all the work. We must be willing to do whatever God asks of us in our healing process. He's waiting for us to do so. Let's do it today. Let's believe and have faith in our linens of waiting.

Day 2
Linens of Grief

John 11:35 "Jesus wept." (NIV)

It is the shortest verse in the Bible, and yet the most profound. It contains two words and has several implications. How can such a brief statement have such an impact on us as believers?

Read and record John 11:35.

Why do you think God puts this verse in His Word?

What does this verse mean to you personally?

Here we have the Scripture that Lazarus has died. Jesus has stayed away when he heard that Lazarus was sick. Then Lazarus dies. Jesus goes a couple of days later and Lazarus' sisters tell him that Lazarus has died.

Read John 11:32-35.

The verses leading up to when Jesus wept are important. Notice in verse 32 that Mary falls at Jesus' feet and says, *"Lord, if you had been here, my brother would not have died." (NIV)* Mary does this out of sincerity.

Notice her physical position. Many scholars will tell you Mary fell at Jesus' feet out of a sign of Lordship. However, I believe there is also another reason.

What could be another reason Mary fell at Jesus' feet?

I believe another reason Mary fell at Jesus' feet when he arrived in Bethany was because of this: she was desperate and in need. Desperate to somehow show her pain-stricken emotions of grief. Mary could have hugged Jesus but she didn't. Christ arrives on the scene and Mary probably ran to him and just fell down in severe anguish.

Have you ever been so grieved that you fell down in your emotions?

What was the situation? Please share with the group if you are comfortable.

Read and record John 11:34a

After Mary falls at Jesus' feet in deep grief the Scripture says demonstrates again that Jesus was aware of her weeping as well as the Jews who were with her.

Why do you think God's verse reiterates this theme of weeping?

I believe there is an underlying theme of weeping and grief and that God want to make sure we understand that Jesus was and is compassionate to our needs in times when we need comforting after the loss of a loved one.

Look up the following verses on God's compassion:

Psalm 145:8

Exodus 22:27

Lamentations 3:22

2 Chronicles 30:9

The verse leading up to Jesus weeping shows us the compassion that He has upon us. He physically saw Mary weeping as well as the other Jews who loved Lazarus. He too loved Lazarus. It also says that when Jesus saw them weeping *"he was deeply moved in spirit and troubled." (NIV)*

What do you think this verse means?

Do you think the Creator of Life, Jesus Christ, was troubled by death and the reality all of us will face someday and the fact He would very soon be going to the cross for the release of us from death? Or was He troubled that Lazarus was no longer there to break bread with, laugh with, and swap stories with? Maybe Jesus was troubled because the friendship had ceased to be and it would not be until He had suffered until the problem would be rectified.

The next verse gives us great insight into God's heart. It says *"Jesus wept."* *(v.35)*

This is one of my two favorite verses in all God's Word. Why? Because it shows us God's humanness. Jesus wept and cried just like we do. Just like Mary and Martha and the Jews were doing. Even though Jesus was about to raise Lazarus from the dead He went ahead and showed his very human emotions. Why? To let us know that He knows how we feel in times of grief. I call this the 'linens of grief.' God didn't have a flippant attitude of "well, I'm going to raise Lazarus from the dead and these people are weeping for nothing." No, Jesus wept *along* with them. He is there for us in our time of need. He is our comforter. Can God not comprehend and understand our brokenness and our humanness? Think our issues or emotions keep us at bay from a loving God? Whenever we feel isolated in our wounds, let us remember that Jesus wept. He wept for us. He wept to demonstrate how much He is like us. He understands our predicament. Take heart friend, we have a God who has been there.

Day 3
Linens of Life

2 Timothy 1:10 "…Christ Jesus, who has destroyed death and has brought life and immortality to light through the gospel." (NIV)

What does life mean to you?

What is the most important thing in life to you? Why?

Look up and record John 14:6

I tried for years to find meaning in many things. I was a tennis player and practiced an ungodly amount of time. The hard work paid off and I was ranked number one in Arkansas from the time I was twelve until I was eighteen. I was ranked highly in the South as well as nationally. I went to a division one college on a full tennis scholarship. I thought if I could just win enough matches then maybe I would find purpose and meaning in my life. Guess what? It didn't. I got a college education but no meaning of life. This was *after* I was a believer.

Sometimes I wrongly think we are urged to come to Christ to have Him take away all our problems. Yes, He is the answer to anything, but I don't believe that God just instantly takes away all our issues. After all, we are human. Even as Christians we will still struggle. I struggled with bulimia for almost twenty years. When I accepted Christ He did not magically take away my eating disorder. Yes, He convicted me of it and the untold damage that it was doing on my body but He didn't cure me in an instant. And so I believe that is the case when we have been wounded. Can He heal us? Without a doubt He can. But many times we have a very large part in our healing of certain addictions or issues.

Is there an area you have been afraid to give over to God?

How has this impacted your life?

Jesus said He was *"the way, the truth, and the life." (John 14:6, NIV)* If we are ever to find the true meaning and happiness of life, then we must give God everything. This means after we become believers. It is a continual process. If we are ever to heal from our past hurts then giving Him those hurts, whether in the form of an addiction or not, must be explored. We may not can do it overnight, but rest assured He will help us on our journey of healing. I didn't give Him my tennis until I was a junior in college. I still got up at 5:30am to practice and I still lifted weights, ran, and played countless hours of tennis every day, but I gave the meaning of it over to Him. Over a period of time. I didn't just wake up and do it. It took time. As for the bulimia, I didn't get in recovery until I was in my mid-thirties. It's funny, but my eating disorder and tennis addiction was my feeble attempt to control things when things had been so out of my control when I was younger. So giving God the control was a whole new concept for me.

Why do you think giving God complete control over our lives is so hard?

Do you think it is a one time event such as when we become believers? Why or why not?

Life is all about Christ and our life in Him. Until we continually make Him Lord of our lives each day then we will attempt to find meaning in other things or people. In work, sports, eating, relationships, addictions, etc. We can make Him our Savior once and be secure eternally with this decision, but making Him Lord of our lives requires constant reassessing each day. We won't be perfect. God doesn't expect us to be perfect. But He does make it fruitless if we look for our life meaning outside of Him. I call this "linens of life." He has designed it so we need Him each day of our lives in order to experience the fruits of the spirit.

Look up the following verses and record:

Colossians 3:3

Romans 6:13

Deuteronomy 30:15

John 11:43 "Jesus called in a loud voice, Lazarus, come out! The dead man came out…"(NIV)

Do you see any similarities between Lazarus and us? What?

Are we not all dead in some way or manner? It may be we are dead in our sins until we accept Christ, or, if we are believers we may be dead in the way we try to fill up our lives and find meaning outside of Christ. Either way, we need a compassionate God who will rescue us from the muck and mire of our own doing. Without the healing balm of Jesus, we will struggle to find meaning apart from Him and all His ways. If Christ is truly the life and therefore meaning in this world, we will not find anything close to happiness apart from giving Him our lives…that means giving Him all our hurts from the past. Today, if you hear His voice, listen to that still sound…or maybe it is a foghorn. Either way, let go and tell Him all about your pain. Things may not change overnight, but they will change in God's timing. All it takes is our cooperation. He'll do all the rest. He'll miraculously send people into our lives to help us heal. That's a life I'm looking forward to. One of meaning and fulfillment. A life full of Christ.

Day 4
Linens of Realness

Colossians 2:17b "…the reality, however, is found in Christ." (NIV)

How do you define 'realness?'

Do you enjoy being around other Christians who are real? Why or why not?

I don't know about you but I love being around 'reality based' Christians. You know what I'm talking about. The ones who aren't afraid to tell you or others in a Bible study that they feel like worm dirt. Or better yet, the ones who bare a little bit of their soul as a very human believer. I have been in Bible studies before where such real sharing was not encouraged. For example, if Mary Sue had a bad day and told the group about it, then the leader judged or looked down on Mary Sue because she wasn't more "spiritual." I believe those leaders or groups that encourage super spirituality do a great disservice to the rest of us who are very human and mess up royally each week…or each day. I'm not saying that we should spill our guts to all Bible studies or friends, but I do highly recommend that we be a part of a group or relationship that is honest, caring, and compassionate. Such relationships are the true body of Christ I believe.

The story of Lazarus is a story of 'realness.' What do you think is meant by this? Please share with the group if you feel comfortable.

Can you imagine being God (take that in for a moment will you), and having the myriads of angels encircling your throne and bowing down to you and you decide to skip out on the place and venture down to the earth trodden planet where sin, death, suffering, and trials await you before you take back your entitlement home. Kinda sounds insane doesn't it? But, as we know, it happened. Jesus came down to earth to not merely shout and say 'I understand,' but rather to whisper and say *'I know.'*

Why do you think Jesus left perfection to come down here to us?

What did He give up in your estimation?

What common things do we have in Christ when He decided to venture to earth?

It can be said that the Gospel is a story about real love. A real love that cared enough for you and me to save us from sin and from ourselves and others. A real love with real needs.

What needs did Jesus have while He was on earth?

Doesn't it blow your mind that Jesus went through the same emotions, such as weeping, sadness, grief, suffering, joy, etc. that we go through? And oh yes, He was tempted in every way we were…but He dodged that bullet whereas we give in many times. Jesus, God Incarnate, had real needs. After all, He was a real person in flesh and blood. He needed food, water, shelter, relationships, and so on. He was the bread of life but He needed food on a daily basis. He was the resurrection but needed a real body to live in.

He was the truth, but had to endure real lies about him from others. He was the life, but died a real death. It all sounds so ironic doesn't it?

What is the one thing God desires of us you think?

Honesty. Without it we are doomed from the start. Yes, we are to love and be obedient to God. But can we do that without getting honest with Him? "I'll love that person….but I really hate her." "I'll do it…but I really don't want to." I believe in order to love and obey God we have to get real and honest before He can do a real work in us. What good is being a robot of faith if we don't trust God enough to be real with Him?

Do you think the world encourages realness? Why or why not?

Do you think the church encourages realness? Why or why not?

The story of Christ is a story about realness. A real live human Savior. A real cross. Real suffering. Real death.

Look up and record the following verses:

Philippians 2:8

Colossians 1:10

Hebrews 12:2

Jesus suffered greatly for us. It says in Isaiah that Christ was beaten beyond recognition. Not just crucified, but beaten where He was unrecognizable if you didn't know it was Him on the cross. Now that's real pain and suffering. Why? Because He knew we needed a real Savior who knows what it is like to have insomnia. What it is like to wake up hungry. What it is like to lose a loved one. What it is like to feel all alone. Wouldn't we rather come to this kind of a Savior and God rather than a super spiritual one who cannot grasp our trials and tribulations while here on earth?

I encourage you to look again at the story of Lazarus. I think you will find a real God who wanted to demonstrate His realness by weeping first before He raised His friend from the dead. He didn't have to cry you know. But Jesus is like that. So real and honest. Don't you think it is time we established relationships with others as well as with Him based on truth of our issues or struggles or emotions rather than putting on a happy face and lying to God and others about how spiritual we feel? God desires linens of realness. I'm going to wrap myself in those garments today and see what God has in store for me. I think you'll be glad you did too.

Debbie Vanderslice

Day 5
Linens of Freedom

2 Corinthians 3:17 "Now the Lord is the Spirit, and where the Spirit of the Lord is, there is freedom." (NIV)

Read John 11 43-44

Why didn't Jesus just take off or make Lazarus' linens or grave clothes come off?

What can we learn from this very important point made by Christ?

It is just a fact. We all have grave clothes. We all have issues that keep us from living the life God has called for us...a life of freedom in Him. Because there is sin in the world, we will all struggle with certain things in our lives. That's the story of Lazarus. He needed help from others in taking off those old grave clothes, or death clothes if you will, before He could live again. Jesus didn't just say "Hey, help him out will you?" No, Jesus commanded others to help him specifically take off what was hindering him from living the Christian life.

Do we owe others our help if we are able to help them with their grave clothes? Why or why not?

I'm not saying we have to be a rescuer or anything that is unhealthy. I'm just saying that God commands us to help when we can. Sometimes we can't. Other times we can. Maybe it's just offering a word of encouragement. Maybe it's buying someone a meal. The list can go on and on. How God specifically uses us is up to Him. We are His vessels. We never know when it will come our time to need help with our grave clothes.

It is interesting that God uses the word freedom to describe the life of Christ and what we have in Him.

Look up the following verses and record:

Luke 4:18

Isaiah 61:1

It is no accident that Lazarus was bound up, just like a prisoner, when he was healed. Yes, Lazarus was healed, much like we are healed spiritually when we become a Christian, but was still in bondage until others helped him take off his grave clothes. We can be a believer but still be in bondage.

Is there anything you are in bondage with today?

What can you do about it?

Do you see anyone who you might could help with their grave clothes?

Are you reluctant to help? Why?

You don't have to have your life all together or be perfect to help someone else with their grave clothes. Just a willing heart and an open mind. This is ingredient #3, Our Responsibility to Others. In our recovery to be healed by the balm of Gilead, nothing can heal our hurts like opening our lives to help others in the same or similar areas we have had issues in. Not rescuing them, but helping maybe peel a layer or two of something that keeps them from being all God has called them to be. Thank God for Lazarus being bound up. I need a Savior who knew I needed others to help me out of my bondage. True freedom comes from Christ and somehow He knew we might need others.

Prayer: Dear God, thank you for coming to earth to be real for us, especially in our times of need. Give us the courage and faith to get help when we need it from others when we are in need of taking off our grave clothes. Let us help others with their death linens as well when we are able to do so. Help us to take our healing one day at a time as we seek you for restoration. In Jesus' name, Amen.

Write out your prayer below in the space provided.

CHAPTER 4

Mirror Mirror on the Wall

(Ingredient #4 Believing What is Fact Instead of What We Feel)

Day 1
Mirrors Lie

I Corinthians 13:12 "Now we see but a poor reflection as in a mirror..."(NIV)

This chapter takes into account what all of us have done from time to time...believe what we feel instead of what is actually fact. Because we are only human, we will all struggle at some point in our lives with our feelings instead of what is actually true. When we are able to separate the two, true healing begins to seep into our lives as medicine for our heartbroken souls.

There is a mirror that looks like you but it distorts the truth. Instead of giving you reality it gives a false representation of yourself. You are either very skinny or very fat.

Why is there no reality based mirror?

Who would pay money to see a real mirror…we can see that at home.

I call it "a codependent mirror." I don't know many women who love their figure.

Me included.

Sometimes we try to trick ourselves into the truth while never admitting the lie we have behind us.

Who is called the father of lies.

Read John 8:44-45

Why do we believe Satan over God and His word?

Why do we believe lies about ourselves instead of how God sees us?

How does God see us?

Read and record Psalm 34:5

No matter our sins or mistakes God sees us as bright and radiant

What do you think of when you hear the word "radiant?"

When He sees us He sees Christ-pure, spotless, and radiant. No matter what the county fair mirrors say. Or anyone for that matter.

When we look to Him, He responds by living His life through us and He sees something beautiful. Let's not look to the county fair and its house of mirrors. Let's look to the cross instead!

Day 2
You've Lost that Loving Feeling

Philippians 3:8 ...for whose sake I have lost all things..." (NIV)

When we stand before our family and friends and God, we promise to forsake all others, love and cherish each other until death. That's the easy part. The consummation part is the fun and easy part. But living our marriage out from day to day is the real challenge.

l. Romans 1:25

2. Titus 1:2

3 Hebrews 6:8

I believe that there should be a mandatory waiting period of ten years before marriage. All kidding aside, I like Tom Hanks when he played Forest Gump and said "life is like a box of chocolates. You don't know what you're going to get until you open the box and bite into one of them."

Day 3
Reality Sets In

Colossians 2:17 "These are a shadow of things that were to come, the reality, however, is found in Christ." (NIV)

Read and record Jeremiah 8:22What does it say?

Gilead was the healing mecca of Biblical times, much like Hot Springs, Arkansas was in the 1930's.

Why are some people healed and others are not?

There are some people that think if you are "super spiritual" you will be healed of anything. However this "coke machine theology leaves God out of the picture. In goes the request of healing and out comes the desired healing. However this mentality leaves God out of the picture. It becomes all about them and their activity. This can lead to spiritual snobbery.

My God cannot be put in a box. If He were in a box, then we would have to discount all the Biblical heroes who were very flawed. Below is just a few of the men and women who were greatly used by God in spite of their very sin riddled lives.

David

Paul

Bathsheba

The woman who bled for 12 years

The woman at the well

Mary Magdalene

Tamar

If God can use them, then surely He can use us? Are you feeling a little bit better friend. I hope so.

Day 4
Don't Go Down that Road

"Luke 3:5 …crooked roads shall become straight."(NIV)

Gilead was the healing mecca like Hot Springs, Arkansas was in the 1930's.

FDR, the president, was said to have visited the springs for his handicap. He said it helped him profusely.

Looks can be deceiving. While we are earnestly seeking God, Satan may throw any barrier our way to deter us from becoming all we can be.

Are there any barriers in your life?

If so, what is your game plan?

We are bombarded with choices everyday If you doubt this just turn on the television. Even the T.V. evangelical preachers are trying to "sell God" by saying "Give your soul to God but send your money to us." Sad but true.

Look up and record the following verses:

Matthew 7:13

Luke 3:5

What do these verses say to you?

I know I am repeating myself read and record John 8;32 What does it say?

The Greek word for "to know" means to know as in consummation of marriage. That requires action as in doing.

For example, I can theoretically know I am an alcoholic, but until I do something with that truth I will remain in bondage. Roads can hinder or help. Help get us to our destination. Hinder if there is a road side bomb awaiting us. It's up to us to decipher which road to go down.

How will we know which fork in the road to take? That's easy

What does God's word say?

What do the wisest people say?

And sleep on it. I personally am the most impatient person….and driver. I hate for other people in the car to drive…with me in charge we will arrive much sooner.

When we see a traffic sign that says "do not enter or bridge out" we need to obey the sign or there might be trouble ahead of us, not to mention in our rear view mirror.

Why then would we not obey God's Word for us? It, not obeying God's Word only leads to trouble.

Give an example of when you disobeyed God's Word?

How did it affect you?

Day 5
The Ultimate Mirror

2Corinthians 5:7 "We live by faith and not by sight." (NIV)

Read and record Colossians 2:17-18

What does it say?

Who is our reality?

The ultimate mirror is Christ. When He looks at us He sees Christ in us. We don't do anything on our own, but rather it is Him living through us.

Read and record Eph. 3:20

What does it say?

We are to do God's work while we are here on earth. God Works through us to accomplish His divine purposes. How cool is that?!We help Him through the salvation and growth process. How cool is that?! It is not us doing it but rather God working through us.

Prayer: Help us Lord to decipher between good and evil. Help us to know what is false and what isn't and the way we feel. May our actions be indicative of you and you alone.

Write out your prayer in the space provided below.

PART II

LIVING IN THE PRESENT

CHAPTER 5

A Trip to the Dentist

(Ingredient #5 Believing We Can Apply Medicine as Deep as the Wound Goes)

Jeremiah 46:11 "Go up to Gilead and get balm, O Virgin Daughter of Egypt. But you multiply remedies in vain; there is no healing for you"(NIV)

Day 1
The Bed of Pain

Job 6:10b "Then I would have still have this consolation- my joy in unrelenting pain...NIV)..."

Lay down upon this bed of pain

The sorrows deep you can't contain.

I come gently to tuck you in

And hold you close from evil's den.

Though your hurt is a well dug deep

I'll soften your pillow so you will sleep.

The bliss of peace will overflow

My healing love you will know.

Sleep well with this longing of mine,

For I'm the bliss you will find.

Debbie Vanderslice (2010 New Hope Publishers, Shameless p.93)

What is your bed of pain?

What have you done with that pain?

Is it working or not. If not why not?

Is it 'fixable'? If not why not?

What is your longing? Be specific.

C.S. Lewis said that "pain is God's megaphone. If that is the case, what is He saying to you?

Read and record John 8;32

It does not say some things work together for good, but rather ALL things work together for good for those who love God and are called according to His Purpose.

Who benefits this?

We all are mighty fortunate. God can take any situation and turn it into good. Now, that's a loving God.

Please share with the group how God has turned something bad into good.

Day 2
X-Rays Don't Lie

Titus 1;2 ...which God, who does not lie." (NIV)

Does God ever lie?

Who is the father of lies.

Look up the following verses:

Numbers 23:19

1Timothy 3:9

1Timothy 4:6

John 3:33

Titus :1:2

When God promises something, it is a done deal. Take it to the bank promise. We live in a world of broken vows and promises. If that is all we know, then trusting God can be difficult.

Do you have trouble trusting God?

Why or why not.

In what way are trusting God and X-rays alike?

Day 3
Pain Medicine vs. Root Canal

Jeremiah 15:18 'Why is my pain unending"(NIV)

Matthew 3:10

Matthew 13:21

What did all these verses mean to you? What struck you?

I've sat in the dentist chair more than half my life it seems like I've had a dozen or so root canals. So, when I was unable to chew on the right side of my mouth, I knew I needed to see the dentist. The damage was $50 dollars for pulling and $650 for a root canal.

I told him I needed some time to think it over. I went for the extraction. It was a back molar so it was not visible to the naked eye. I opted to have the tooth pulled. He said I should be pain free in a few days

Can pain medicine be a good thing?

What about it being bad?

Pain medicine can be a good thing if used properly. For example, if I have a headache then Tylenol will help. However, if I take hydrocodone for the pain, I may become an addict. I speak from experience on this one.

There is a difference between a little bit of pain vs. a lot of pain. Don't become a statistic.

Root canals get down to the root of the problem. Pain meds do not. X-Rays don't lie. Get out of the shadows and into the light,

Read and record the following verses:

John 1:5

Psalm 91:1

Isaiah 51:16

What do these verses say?

Read and record the following verses:

Job 6:10

Job 6:25

1Thess. 5:3

I don't know about you, but it feels so much better to be in the light than in the dark shadows, like where the root canals live.

Day 4
The Numbing Needle

John 8:32 "You shall know the truth and the truth shall set you free. (NIV)

I sat uncomfortably in the cold, vinyl chair in my dentist office. I had been unable to chew on the left side of my mouth. "Probably a root canal, or a cavity," I mumbled to myself. Finally, the dentist came in to deliver the news. I had an abscessed molar that had once been a root canal, but now had developed into a more serious condition.

As I looked at the film, the dentist pointed out the darkness, or shadows, where the abscessed tooth was. "But didn't the root canal work?" I asked. "Well, the medicine we applied didn't go deep enough into the wound." "Don't worry, you'll be getting a numbing needle soon." The real truth is called a shot.

Have you ever gotten a numbing needle at the dentist office?

Did you enjoy it?

How did it make you feel?

Suddenly a light bulb went off in my head. "That's it," I said to myself. "I've been applying medicine, but not deep enough to heal the wounds of my life." I was afraid to go all the way inside the wounds. The pain would kill me. Or so I thought.

If you are anything like me, you avoid pain like the plague. When I had my daughter, I went into the hospital with open arms for all the drugs they could muster for childbirth. It's interesting, but my dentist prescribed not only an antibiotic to heal my abscessed tooth, but also a pain medication. The infection had made my entire body sick, thus I needed an antibiotic. To mask the pain I took pain killers. I would feel nothing

Is there anything you mask to avoid pain?

It does not have to be drugs, it could be sports, food, or even lots of bible studies. What do you do in order to avoid spiritual, physical, or emotional pain? Please explain.

Can pain medicine be good? Please explain

Can it be a bad thing? Please explain.

Day 5
Out of Pain into Glory

"Pain is God's Megaphone." (C.S.Lewis The Problem of Pain)

One particular hurt in my life has been the death of my best friend, Martha. Martha was only thirty when she died. After running her first ever dreamed about marathon. Martha was diagnosed with lymphoma cancer.

I had grown particularly close to Martha, my prayer partner. You might find this amazing, but at age twenty- eight she was my first real best friend. Because I was so involved with my tennis and travelling all over the nation, I missed a lot of school and social functions. I invested my life with tennis until Martha came along.

Were you ever so serious with a hobby or sport that you missed school and school functions?

How did it make you feel?

Martha was visibly many months pregnant with her first child when I met her in a Bible study She came in late and slipped in the back row where I lived and was most comfortable. After the study was over we struck up a conversation. She was due in July and my husband and I were trying. I found Martha to be quite encouraging. Soon we met for breakfast and I told her my good news; I was pregnant. Before I could get back home she had delivered a basket of muffins for me. I quickly found out she was a gift giver like me. A friendship was born.

Do you have a best friend? What is he/she like?

Why is she/he your best friend?

What friendships are you cultivating?

Martha and I spent time talking and eventually became prayer partners. We shared our dreams, struggles, and life philosophies with each other. We were both former athletes who craved art. Martha eventually taught art out of my home after her first child was born.

Martha encouraged me on down days, lifted me up in prayers, and challenged me as a believer. Thus, when she was diagnosed with cancer, my world went into slow motion. I had lots of questions for God as well as anger.

Has your world ever gone into slow motion?" Please explain

During Martha's illness, we became closer. I helped babysit her son as well as spent time with Martha praying. I even spent nights in the hospital when Martha was terminal. During Martha's final days something miraculous happened. I was drawn to Martha like a moth to the flame. As her body failed, her spirit soared. While Martha faded away, Christ in her shone through. When our bodies and minds slowly go, our souls and spirits remain.

Have you ever experienced this miracle of death or dying?

Please explain.

In her final days, I read the Psalms to Martha. We talked about God and as she prepare to leave behind many many people who loved her dearly. First I prayed for Martha's complete healing. It didn't come. Then I prayed for the rapture. It didn't come. Next I prayed to be taken first so I would be spared the pain of losing my friend. It didn't happen. It was a bitter pill to swallow at such a young age.

When Martha died, I was left with two options. Draw close to God or get away. I chose the latter. I cursed God, gave Him the proverbial finger, and stayed very far away.

What was your reaction to someone close to you that died? Please explain.

Perhaps you can relate to the poem I wrote below.

The Friendship Tears

I come to you with

Unashamed friendship tears to weep.

You never tell me to stem them,

Only to pour them at your feet.

She was a light down here

For just a short while.

I never dreamed the race she would run

On behalf of Heaven's mile.

Tenderness, touch, and trust

Were ours indeed to share.

You freed my soul to love

As it was brokenly laid bare.

Many years ago I asked you

What friendship was all about

You opened Heaven's graceful gate

And whispered Martha's name with evidence of a shout

So deaf did I become

As I begged for time to keep.

"This my precious child is proof of my love for you because I have given you freedom with friendship tears to weep.(Shameless, 2008, New Hope Publishers p. 49)

Prayer: Won't we allow The Great Physician to apply His balm as deep and wide our wounds are. I will end this chapter by giving you my favorite movie character. In the words of Percy from The Spitfire Grill." Sometimes the handling of a wound can hurt worse than the wound itself." Amen

Please use the space below to write out your own prayer:

CHAPTER 6

The Rain Gauge Renaissance

Ingredient #6 Believing We Can Stand Firmly in the Present One Day at a Time While Putting the Past into Proper Perspective.

Day 1
Storms

Luke 21:19 By standing firm you will gain life." (NIV)

The storm raged on. Drop after drop the down-pour announced its' arrival and assault on the fallow ground. People scurried to and fro for shelter from the rain. It was as if the heavens opened their gates and let the tears of the angels fall for all the years the saints had endured heartache. Then as quickly as it had started, it stopped. I slowly sauntered out of my house to access the damage. Trees were down, power lines snapped in two, and debris literally littered the neighborhood.

Describe the worst storm you have ever been in. What happened?

What was or is the worst storm you have ever been in?

The worst storm I was ever in happened when I was about nine years old. My Mom and Dad were at work and my older sister and I were at home. We got in the basement and at the height of the tornado, the doorbell rang. My sister made me promise that I would not go upstairs. At the door were my grandmother and grandfather. My 80 year old grandmother, Mame, got on the floor and prayed for our safety. It remains my most vivid memory of my grandmother.

Read and record Job 38:1

It says that the Lord answered Job from the whirlwind.

Why is that in scripture?

It means that God speaks to us in the midst of our storms.

What storms are you currently going through?

If we didn't have storms in our lives, then God cannot do His great work through us.

Read and record Malachi 3:2 What does it say?

There is a certain denomination that teaches what I call the "coke machine" mentality. In goes the prayer request and out comes the desired result. But God loves us too much and refines us through our sicknesses and tribulations. If we never struggled or had pain, how could we grow?

I wish I could write about "fluff" Biblical mentality but I can't. I am a very fallible human being whose hope is in God alone. When I am left to my own devices I end up with a bad frame of mind. I have a totally different demeanor if I spend time with God first thing in the morning. Heaven help the world if I don't. Especially during rush hour traffic

Day 2
The Rain Gauge Renaissance

Job 38:1 "The Lord answered Job out of the storm." (NIV)

There, stuck into the ground, was the tell-tale sign of the storm: the rain gauge. Its' top overflowed and I bent down to empty it. "Darn I forgot to empty it out from the last rain we'd had, as I berated myself for forgetting. Now, I didn't know how much rain we'd really had.

Look up the following verses and record in the space provided below:

Deuteronomy 25:14

Jeremiah 31:37

Isaiah 40:12

What do all these verses have in common?

As if a brick had hit me in the head, I felt God's insight on the stupid little rain gauge incident or Renaissance. The renaissance was the transitional movement in Europe between 14th and 17th century expressed through the arts, literature and sciences. (.Webster's online dictionary) It was an awakening of sorts. The renaissance rain was mixed together, past rains and present rains. Although it, the rain gauge, was intended to measure the most recent rain, life had gotten in the way and I had forgotten to empty it. It had measured both the present and past rain.

What good was the past rain?

Although I am not advocating into always looking at our past, I am encouraging us to think about our lives as a rain-gauge, one that mixes together both the present as well as the past. However, like all rain gauges we must continually empty out the past in order to better adhere and measure the present.

What would you call The Rain Gauge Renaissance? Describe it in your own words

One particular struggle I have had is to move forward from my friend, Martha's death. I won't lie. It, grieving, has been overwhelming.

At one point when Martha slipped into a coma one Sunday morning in late July, I kept asking myself, "When are the adults going to get here? When is it going to get better?"

It took me over a five hour time period that we were the adults. At age 29, I thought security in life and death situations came with older adults. Not so, I found out. It's still a hard row to hoe.

Have you been there friend?

Did your life suddenly go into a swirling tornado? Please share with the group if you feel comfortable.

Have you ever been in a life and death situation? If you have please explain.

Day 3
The Past

Isaiah 43:18…do not dwell on the past." (NIV)

I have not been standing firmly in the present I must admit.

Record Isaiah 43:18

This is one of my favorite verses. It gives me hope…mainly when I mess up a time or two.

What does this verse mean to you?

I think of a very true statement. "When Satan reminds you of your past, remind him of his future…the lake of fire!

Now if I could do that I'd be in great shape. We are only human when we dig up the old dog bone. He wants us to know that He is doing "new things" for us. If only I had listened to Him the first time! I've learned that everyone has a past and things that are not too Godly. Beware of two kinds of people:

People who never struggle

And people who judge others for being very fallible

Read and record Romans 15:4

What two things were the scriptures written for?

The past does NOT define us. It is through Christ we have been redeemed. Our forgiveness is not with man but rather with God. He is our ultimate judge. Not man nor a church or pastor. God and God alone.

Why did Christ come?

Read and record Exodus 24:8

Read and record Romans 3:25

Revelation 1:5

Day 4
The Present

Hebrews 12:1 Therefore, since we are surrounded by such a great cloud of witnesses, let us throw off everything that hinders and the sin that so easily entangles, and let us run with perseverance the race marked out for us" (NIV)

Do you think that there is a specific race we have to run for Christ? If so, please explain.

Do you think we can change? I've heard it say that a leopard cannot change his spots. What do you think about that?

I believe no one is so far removed from God that they cannot be redeemed. If you can name it, the sin, God can forgive it.

No matter our struggles even if we come to Jesus with the same sin or addiction, Christ will forgive us. No matter what. That is why Jesus came. To bridge the gap so we could have eternal life.

It is up to us if we will cross Christ's bridge or not.

One verse I love when I dig up old dog bones, or past sins, is the following.

2 Corinthians 5:17. What does it say?

When I wake up each day I pray to God these three things:

Thank you for this day

Give me the strength to do your will.

Help me see you in the lives of others

There have been days, weeks, and years when I did zilch on these three things. Thank God He grades on the curve!

Look up the following verses and share with the group what each means to you.

1 Corinthians 3:22

1 Timothy 4:8

Look up Jeremiah 8:22 and record.

Gilead back in Biblical times was what Hot Springs, Arkansas was in the 1930's Both are said to have had healing properties in the water. Franklin D. Roosevelt visited the hot springs in search of relief from his polio adversities. People still flock to Hot Springs with a myriad of ailments.

Is there anything that needs healing in your life?

The hardest part for me is to move forward in spite of the past. It doesn't mean I will forget Martha, just the opposite –emptying old rain, out of the rain gauge. Does this make my memories of Martha less clear? No. Does this mean I love her less? Of course not. It simply means I must live in the present to enjoy today's shower of love.

What does "the balm in Gilead" mean to you personally?

What does the phase "shower of love" mean to you?

If Martha were here she would be angry at me. She'd say something along these lines: "Deb, why on earth have you mourned me for over a decade. Enough already, move on."

Today, if I were to talk about her I would cry. It's getting better however. The more God cleans out my fear of abandonment, the more likely I am to cultivate friendship.

Is it scary? Yes. Do I second guess myself? All the time. But, with God's grace and help, and the reality of taking it one day at a time, I'm slowly healing and moving forward. By allowing others to be the healing balm in my life in regard to friendships, I am slowly getting to the roots that have caused so much pain.

As I empty yesterday's rain gauge, I am reminded of the sweetness as well as sorrow I experienced. But today is a new day. I must stand firmly in the present or else that which happens today will be a blur and be recorded in yesterday's rain gauge. I don't want to miss it. The miracle of today. The presence of today.

What does Matthew 6:11 say? Please record.

It is the Lord's Prayer. He says "give us today our daily bread," He doesn't say "eat yesterday's bread or I'll feed you tomorrow." No, God Incarnate, in all His wisdom gives us exactly what we need; today's bread.

Why does God do this?

I believe that if you live in the past, and rely upon past predicaments, that we will get stuck and not move forward in the sanctifying process. I also believe that the future is worth striving for, but if all we do is look ahead, we forget the daily part of living. The past and future are reminders, or markers. The past does not define us as we are God's children. Neither does the future predict with accuracy what we will become. All we can do is put one foot in front of the other and eat our daily bread.

Day 5
The Future

Jeremiah 29:11, "plans to give you a hope and a future." (NIV)

Read and record the following:

2Samuel 22:31

Psalm 18:30

2Corinthians 12:9

Read Genesis 19

What do these verses mean to you? Please explain

This reminds me of a story that I believe God purposely put in the bible for us to learn from. The premise is simple. God is going to destroy the sinful cities of Sodom and Gomorrah. Lot and his wife are to flee the cities and to not turn back and look at the destruction. God is very clear with his instructions. However curiosity gets the best of Lot's wife and she is turned into a pillar of salt.

At first glance we may think God is being too harsh. But hold on, by looking back, Lot's wife is reminded of all she is losing instead of striving for the future she is gaining. She loses her life not because of disobedience to God but because she yearned for yester-year, when in fact God had something better down the road.

How many times are we like Lot's wife? More than I care to admit.

We're not going to be perfect. Sometimes we will forget to empty yesterday's rain out of the rain gauge. But that's ok. We are not perfect people. We will slip up and fall. Some of us will stay stuck for nine years like I did. But that's ok too. It is what it is. God's timing is perfect. Let's allow God to send His healing balm of living in the present, although the past will occasionally get mixed in. We do this on day at a time. Won't you allow the balm of Gilead to guide you just for today? You'll be glad you did!

Prayer: Dear God, help us to keep our eyes on Christ so we won't miss any blessings you have for us. In Christ's holy and perfect ways. Amen

Write your prayer below:

CHAPTER 7

The Promise of Satisfaction

(Ingredient #7 Believing We Can Be Satisfied in Today's World)

Day 1
Satisfaction for Sure

"I can't get no satisfaction" (The Rolling Stones)

My idea of being totally satisfied is to have my tummy full of chicken fahitas, a large Diet Coke, and a ton of cheese dip. Also my entire family is there. Oh it has to be On The Border

Read and record the following verses: What do these verses say to you?

Psalm 63:5

Psalm 105:40

Can you imagine getting bread from heaven and quail as well?

There has been much speculation that the manna was something like a wafer but I disagree. I think it was like a type of bread. There is nothing like a piece of hot bread out of the oven. It had to be good if it was heaven sent.

What do you think the manna was like?

What about the quail?

Read and record Psalm 107:9

God uses the words that satisfies and fills. Those aren't there just for reading. Our two most basic needs….food and water…are cited in the verse.

Why do you think God put them there?

Those two most basic needs must be fulfilled according to Maslow's hierarchy. We really can't do anything without these two needs being met.

What are some other needs that we need?

At the top of the pyramid is self actualization. This is where we have our goals or dreams.

What satisfies you?

I love to open my Bible and low and behold I find a verse that speaks to me. I also keep a prayer journal and have all my requests in it. I wait for God to say no, yes, or wait.

Day 2
The Sting of Rejection

Isaiah 53::3a He was despised and rejected by men, a man of sorrows, and familiar with suffering (NIV)

Look up the following verses and record your thoughts on them

Psalm 94:14

Isaiah 53:3

Romans 11:14

What is the opposite of acceptance?

I believe it is rejection. To be rejected because of a certain belief is a lame excuse for not praying for them or buying a meal for them. I think it is the fear of the unknown. Don't let those in authority tell you what you should believe and not believe. Investigate for yourself. Get out your Bible and find out what God has to say in His infallible Word.

But to take someone else's word for it is what I call "reckless" Bible seekers. Don't go on the feelings but rather the truth of what God says.

Read and record 1Corinthians 1:27 What does it say?

Why do we as a society walk away or ignore the very people God uses. God chooses the likes of prostitutes, murderers, the sexually impure, the depressed, those with terminal illnesses and so on.

If we live in this world, we have been rejected. Whether it was in the fifth grade or as an adult with a divorce hanging over your head, God accepts as you are.

Name something that you find hard to get over. Share with the group if you feel like it.

Day 3
Eat, Drink, and Be Merry

Matthew 20, 22 "Can you drink the cup I am going to drink..." (NIV)

Look up the following verses and record them as well

Luke 12:19-21

Philippians 2:17

The verse that says Paul is being poured out like a drink offering really speaks to me.

What does that mean to you?

It means to me that it is not Paul who is undergoing great difficulties, but rather Christ in him. He is being poured out like a drink offering

What does the phrase "drink offering" mean to you?

A drink offering means to be emptied or to drink **all** of its' contents. Paul is ready, willing, and able to die for Christ.

What does that verse mean to you?

Paul knew that there was something better after this life.

Do you believe in the afterlife? Why?

Describe your idea of heaven.

Drinking is our most basic need. If we do not have something to drink, then our bodies will die. It's that simple.

So, if we give God a drink offering, we are giving him our very lives. That's why Paul said his life was being poured out like a drink offering Water is our most basic need.

I think Paul knew he was going to die. What do you think?

Read and record 2Timothy 4:6-7

What does it say? If we all could live like Paul did we'd be doing great. This Christian life is a race. Some of us will enter heaven with a bang, while others will be hopping along to the finish line. Whatever your pace is keep on going. Christ is at the finish line ready to greet you. Won't you join in this endurance race?

Day 4
Whatever the Situation

Philippians 4:12b "I have learned the secret of being content in any situation..."(NIV)

Read and define the following verses

1Timothy 6:8

Philippians 4:11-12

Hebrews 13:5

2Coritnians 12:7

Paul, who was imprisoned for over three years had learned to be content no matter what. He was shipwrecked, beaten, stoned. He endured a lot.

Read Philippians 4:13

What was Paul's secret to living?

Do you think you could have survived all that Paul went through? Why or why not?

I like to think I could be like Paul but I love my pizza and diet cokes too much. It has been said that God never gives you more than you can handle. Do you agree or not. Why or why not?

Name a really bad situation you were in. Share with the group if you feel comfortable

Paul wrote most of the New Testament from a prison cell. What all did he have to struggle against?

Read and record Galatians 2:20-21

With the power of Christ living in me I can do anything. Life is all about Christ. What we "do" with Him is up to us.

What is your purpose here on earth?

What gets you up in the morning?

Nothing is ever wasted in our lives.

Read and record Romans 8:28

It doesn't say some things, but rather ALL things work together for good. Nothing we do is ever wasted. God uses even the bad in our lives and can turn it into good.

What have you been holding back from God? Give God a chance to work out His will for your life.

Day 5
Heaven Sent

Isaiah 40:26 "Lift your eyes and look to the heavens..."(NIV)

If I were God. Let me take that in for a moment. And I had a myriad of angels around me saying "holy, holy, holy, I would never want to leave heaven. Oh, let's don't forget the people bowing down to me. And the all-you-can-eat-buffet. It's a good thing I'm not God. Things would get a little bit out of hand.

What's your idea of heaven here on earth?

Salvation is an insane idea really.

Look up and record the following verses:

1Peter 1:4

1Peter 3:22

2Corinthiands 5:1

Thessalonians 4:16

2Peter 3;13

Which verse spoke to you the most?

Read and record Philippians 3:12-14

If I could just do this verse I would be doing great. But thank God He grades on the curve. I don't know about you but I yearn for the eternal. Sometimes I want heaven. No worries, no problems, no sickness, no money concerns, no being overweight. Well, you get the picture. No, we are only given today. Let's live in today and let the blessings flow. Jesus was heaven sent. When we have a relationship with Christ and nurture that relationship we will find the satisfaction we crave. We were made to have a relationship with him. We may stray and try to find satisfaction in other areas. That's ok. He will wait for us. He's a pretty awesome guy.

Prayer: Dear God, thank you that you alone can satisfy us. Lead us the healing truth that you are the author of being satisfied. Forgive us when we go in the wrong direction of trying to meet this need. In Jesus' name. Amen.

Please write out your prayer below in the space provided

CHAPTER 8

The Promise of Peace

(Ingredient #8 Believing We Can Have Peace on Earth)

Day 1
Who is Peace Found In

Philippians 4:7 "And the peace of God, which transcends all understanding will guard your hearts and minds in Christ Jesus.(NIV)

Peace is relative to every person. My definition of peace is as follows: peace is taking a deep breath and saying and thinking all is ok. I'm ok. I know it's not fancy or very academic, but that is what peace is to me.

As to the question of who peace is found in that is easy. Peace is found in Christ and Him alone.

Read and record Isaiah 9:6

I firmly believe that we try by our own devices to obtain peace any way we can.

Here's a list of things we endure in order to get peace.

Alcohol

Drug addiction

Sexual addiction

Food addiction

Workaholism

Gambling

Sports

This is just a short list of what we will do to avoid emotional pan. They do not offer peace in any form or fashion.

Can you relate to this list? Boy, I sure can.

I did not accept Christ until I was 16. All I did was say three little words to Him. I said, "Jesus come in." It was not anything fancy. Very simple and heartfelt. I didn't say the sinner's prayer. The change was immediate.

I stopped cheating at school. My ranking in tennis skyrocketed. I finally found peace with God. Peace with God is different than peace with your fellow man.

Do you see a difference?

What is it?

People have memories like elephants. They never forget. But God is totally different. He forgives us no matter the sin. Forgets also.

Do you feel unforgiven with a particular sin?

Read and record Psalm 103:14.

God's love never fails and He always forgives us. We are the ones who drag up old bones. Not God.

What old dog bones are you holding on to?

Isn't it time to let them go?

Man may not forgive but God does. Don't let man get in your way. Forgiveness is only three words away

Day 2
What is Peace

1Corinthians 14:33 For God is not a God of disorder but of peace." (NIV)

Here is a list of similar words to peace

Calm

Quiet

Stillness

Tranquility

Silence

Harmony

Serenity

Which word do you like best?

Please tell why.

Look up and define the following verses

Ephesians 2:14

Ephesians 6:15

Philippians 4:7

John 15:27

Which verse did you like the best? I think they were all good.

Peace to me is sighing and saying all is well with my soul.

Peace is not going to the nail shop and sighing "I like it" and being happy about that. I'm talking about being content or having peace that it is going to be ok, no matter the situation.

What is your idea of peace.

Peace is a state of mind. And it is relative.

Won't you try your best to have peace in your life today. It is only one short prayer away.

Day 3
Where is Peace Found

1Peter 3:11…he must seek peace and pursue it (NIV)

Read and record the following verses

Ephesians 2:16

Ephesians 6:15

Phippians 4;7

John 14;27

We look everywhere to find the all elusive peace. Below are some of the places we look.

Relationships

Drugs

Alcohol

Sexual addiction

Workaholism

People pleasing

Sports

Where do you find peace?

The Bible says peace is found in Christ?

It is there, peace, for our getting, but we turn away from it. Why do we do this you think?

I was rushed to the hospital with a stroke, My heart stopped for one minute on two different occasions. The paramedic told my family and friends that he didn't think I'd make it. But here I am. I spent five weeks in the hospital before I was moved to a rehab center.

I had a strange dream while in the hospital. I dream that I was in heaven and my close friend and prayer partner Martha was there. I told her "you've got hair". She laughed. She had freshly cut flowers. I asked where she was going. She said "to see the King, of course." I said "I want to go too. Martha said, "it's not your time yet." End of dream.

Where is peace found you think?

I use to think it was found in my tennis. I was ranked #1 in Arkansas for many years 8th in the south and 57 nationally. I won a scholarship to SMU. I thought peace was found in winning on the tennis court.

Who or what do you find peace in?

Peace is found in Christ and Him alone. He designed us so that we were made for a relationship with Him and Him alone. I can't tell you how much better my tennis got when I gave my life to Christ. Suddenly I had a purpose. That relationship changed my life.

Has a relationship with God changed your life?

Please explain.

Peace is an internal thing. Just look at Paul and all he endured for Christ.

Look up and record Philippians 4:11

Think of the worse case and then think of Paul. He was content no matter the situation. Most of his writing came from a jail cell. Isn't that just like God? He loves the depressed, down trodden, prostitutes, murderers, sexually impure, and so on.

God, no matter the sin, never gives up on us. It goes against his nature.

Day 4
When is Peace Found

Malachi 2:6

"He walked with me in peace." (NIV)

Read and record Philippians 4:11-12

What does that verse mean to you?

What did Paul have to overcome.

Read and record Philippians 4:19

God did not create us to have needs not met. We may confuse needs with wants.

We all need water and food and shelter. Those are our basic needs. When we start wanting cable on our tv that is a want. I only have the basic stations, but I love it. I don't want for more stations. It is not a need, it is a want.

What do you want right now in your life?

I am a firm believer in setting goals.

Are you setting goals for yourself? Why or why not?

Are you visualizing? Why or why not?

The brain does not know the difference between what is real and what is visualized. When I was 17 I tried this out. At night before I want to bed I would visualize playing tennis against a girl and the outcome being me the winner. I did this too when I went to a tournament. That year I finished #2 at the Southern tournament and #57 nationally. I credit visualizing as making the difference; Peace can be found in a relationship with Christ. You're probably going to say no way or I'm trying hard but life is too hard. Hold onto those hard ones. C.S. Lewis said that "Pain is God's megaphone." (The Problem of Pain) I don't know about you but I am deaf.

What do you think of his quote?

Day 5
Why Do We Need Peace

1Peter 3:11 "…he must seek peace and pursue it."(NIV)

Look up and record

Isaiah 53:5

Malachi 2:6

John 14:27

Romans 8:6

1Corinthians 14:33

Ephesians 6:15

Which one is your favorite verse? Why?

They are all so good that I can't choose just one.

Jesus, the Prince of Peace desires for all of us to live at peace with one another. I can't stand it when a hate group marches for their cause. They even get violent. God is a God of peace. He desires that we have it. The first step is to make sure you have Christ in your life. My conversion experience was three little words when I was 17. I simply said "Jesus come in" No grand lights, no angels fell from the sky. Just come in. I didn't even know the sinners prayer In conclusion, peace can be found in Christ. Even on the dark days or years. Simply stay in His word, surround yourself with loving, supportive people and keep in seeking God. He's a real good player when we play hide and seek. He always will find us. Take it to the bank.

Prayer:

Thank you God that you are always with us. Thank you that you are our peace. Help us to live full of you and peace now and in the future. In Jesus' name Amen

Write your own prayer in the space provided below

CHAPTER 9

A Pillar of Salt

(Ingredient #9 Hoping for the Future When Our Past Keeps Coming Up)

Day 1
The Predicament

Genesis 50:20b As for you meant evil against me but God meant it for good…"(EVS Study Bible)

Read Genesis 50

Summarize the chapter.

Can angels masquerade as people?

Look up and record Genesis. 19:1

Scripture seems to suggest that angels do indeed play a part of our lives. Why is it so hard to believe that angels exist?

How many close calls have you had and heard the expression "boy, your angels were watching over you."

Do you believe in angels? Why or why not. Explain your response.

I believe that there are good angels and that there are bad angels. The author, Frank Peretti, does an awesome job with angels and demons and spiritual warfare

Read and record 2Corinthians 1:14

Just like God has his angels, so too does Satan. Don't be a cafeteria Christian…where you pick and choose what you will believe about God. Get out your Bible and decide for yourself.

I believe there are black or dark angels who work for Satan. Then there are good angels who work for God. Angels may disguise themselves as normal. I mean, come on, have you seen any angels in white with wings floating around. God is much smarter than that. They dress the culture and times

Day 2
Angels to the Rescue

Hebrews 13:3b "...some have entertained angels unaware," (ESV)

Read and record Genesis 19:12-13

What role did the angels play?

What exactly did the angels do?

Who did Lot run and tell about the coming doom?

Did everyone take heed about this warning?

Debbie Vanderslice

What would you have done?

What is your definition of an angel?

Psalm 34:7

Day 3
Get Out Now

Genesis 19:14b

"Up! Get out of this place, for the Lord is about to destroy this city" (ESV)

What two cities were going to be destroyed?

What family members went along with Lot?

If you could take anyone with you to avoid a disaster, who would you take? Why?

Who thought it was a joke?

Sometimes we may think someone is joking or kidding around with us. Have you ever done anything in jest only later to get in trouble? If we believe the good news and that Jesus forgives us of our sins He will do just that. That's why He came and died. For forgiveness of our sins. If we dabble a little bit in sin we will have to pay the piped piper.

Have you ever had an encounter with an angel?

Day 4
Destroying the Cities

"by turning the cities of Sodom and Gemorrah to ashes." (2Peter 2:6a ESV Study Bible)

Angels aren't just heavenly beings dressed in a white robe. I doubt the two angels who appeared to Lot were dressed in white robes.

What do you think the angels looked like?

Read and record Genesis 19:12-13

What is going on here?

Who did Lot run and tell to leave?

What does v. 14 say?

Were they in a hurry to 'get out of Dodge?' How do you know?

Who all left the city?

What exactly is a pillar of salt? I think she was turned into a fossil like human. That's just a guess however. What God wants us to see is that she looked back, perhaps thinking of all the things she was losing. God didn't want them looking or living in the past but rather striving for the future.

Safety was found outside the city. What other event was outside the city?

What do you make of that?

Sometimes our redemption takes place outside the norm or familiar.

Change is scary, but let's look at Christ.

When God the Father was in heaven He said I want an acceptable sacrifice. Enter Jesus, the Messiah. Jesus was not like Lot's wife. He saw the future and the prize ahead. In contrast to Lot's wife, she looked back and wanted to live in the past.

Philippians 3:14 What does this verse say?

Let's look ahead for the prize. All around us may be taken from us, but we will always have victory in Christ

Day 5
The Family Line

Genesis 19;29 So it was that when God destroyed the cities of the valley, God remembered Abraham and sent Lot out of the midst of the overthrow when he overthrew the cities in which Lot had lived." (English Standard Version)

Read and Summarize Genesis 19

In your own words what is this passage about?

Was it wrong for Lot's two daughters to become impregnated by him.?

Scripture also says that Lot was drunk when he had sex with his daughters. Scripture says there was no one else was around, that everyone had died in the disaster.

Do these facts make this incest ok? Please explain.

Who took Lot by the hand to get out of the city?

What happened to Lot's wife (v. 26)

At first glance we may think that God was being too harsh on Lot's wife. Maybe she is a reminder that our future lies ahead not behind. Our best days are in the present and future. It does us no good to keep looking at our past and past mistakes.

Prayer: Thank you Father that you do not see only our past mistakes and forgive them, but that you are more interested in our present and future. Thank you for loving us right where are, in the center of your will. In Jesus' name we pray. Amen.

Write your own prayer in the space provided below

CHAPTER 10

A Portrait of Hope

(Ingredient #10 Hoping Against All Hope)

Day 1
Cross Training

Hebrews 12:2

...looking to Jesus, the founder and perfecter of our faith who for the joy set before him endured the cross despising the shame..." (ESV)

Look up and define the following verses:

1Corinthians 9:25

Ephesians 6:4

1Timothy 4:8

2Timothy 3:16

I did a lot of cross training when I was in high school.

This was my schedule, providing that the weather cooperated:

6:30am to 7:30am Drill with my dad

7:30-7:45am Run the bleachers

8-8:30 shower/get ready for school

9am-2pm School

3-5pm Drill with club pro

5:30 Play three sets with various tennis players

7:30 lift weights or go to aerobics

9pm go home, shower, do homework

10pm It would be safe to say that I as a tennis addict. But then it's funny. I accepted Christ when I was 17. It was also at the age that I played my best tennis.

What was the difference? I believe with all my heart that I now had Jesus with me and I also started visualizing.

Do you visualize at all? Why or why not.

Our brain does not know the difference between what is real and what is not real. Olympic athletes work with sport psychologists. If they do it why couldn't I do it?

So before I fell asleep each night I visualized playing tennis and winning and shaking hands with my opponent. I even set goals for myself.

Let's get you going by setting some goals.

Short Range Goals

Now and up to one month

Middle Range Goals

1 month to 6 months

Long Range Goals

6 Months to 1 Year

Also in each category try to have spiritual goals with the same time frame. You might have to think a while but really try to think about where you want to be in terms of spiritual goals. I promise that this will revolutionize your life. Don't quit but stay at it. Try this for 6 months and see what happens. I think you will like the results.

Day 2
The Endurance Race

Luke 21:19 "By your endurance you will gain your lives"(NIV)

Needless to say if I lost a tennis match it was not due to being out of shape. If my opponent beat me they had to hit between 30-40 winners. If they could do that they deserved to win. I was a human backboard. Nobody liked playing me because they knew they would have to be out there all day. Life is not a sprint, it is a marathon. Don't let the down things keep you down.

Since I have run a marathon, I know firsthand how difficult it is. The first 13 miles were a piece of cake. However around mile 20 I had a searing pain in my knee. My split time was 2:20 and I finished with a 5:25. But I didn't walk one step. I ran the whole race.

What kept me going? My love for Martha. My sister appeared around mile 23. I said, "Oh no, a lady who looks just like my sister is coming towards me. Oh it is my sister." I did not recognize her. I was very incoherent.

She and Martha's mom were at the finish line. It, running the marathon, was all about Martha. She was the reason for running the marathon. The fight against cancer was the real marathon.

Read and record the following verses:

Hebrews 12:1-2

2Timothy 7-8

Each of us has a specific race to run. In order to run that race we must get rid of everything that slows us down.

What things or addictions are slowing you down?

Maybe its drugs, alcohol, overeating, starving yourself, people pleasing, sexual addiction. The list can and does go on and on.

What is your weakness?

Day 3
Love Never Fails

1 Corinthians 13;13 So now faith, hope, and love abide, these three; but the greatest of these is love (ESV)

Look up and record 1Corinthians 13:8

What is the greatest of all?

Why do you think love is the greatest?

Love is what God is after in us humans. Love sent Christ to the cross.

What is the greatest thing you have ever done in the name of love?

"When doctors diagnosed my friend Martha as having lymphoma cancer, I was shocked. Not Martha. My Martha. My prayer partner. That was without a one of the most uncontrollable moments in my life. Right then and there I had a choice to make about a situation I had no control over. As I sped over to the hospital that first day, I decided right then and there that I would stay with her through thick and thin by turning closer to God. No matter how bad it got, I would be there for her."

"God drew me to Himself; I was amazed as He poured out His strength –His control on His child. Late one night, I saw Martha witness to a doctor, nurse, and anybody who entered her room. Her spiritual insight was that we are all terminal; we simply don't know it and she did. While Martha wasted away physically, I saw Jesus as never before.

God covered Martha and she delivered her baby daughter-a miracle-Martha witnessed though she wasn't coherent. I saw in essence, Christ poured out as a cup of cold water on a hot August afternoon." (Shameless, New Hope Publishers 2008)

Look up and record Philippians 2:17-1

Author C.S. Lewis in *The Problem of Pain* describes pain as :God's megaphone."

If that is the case then I guess I am deaf. I would have never traded the intimacy I shared with Martha for anything in the world except one thing; Martha to be healed.

It has been many years since Martha died, and I still cry as though it happened yesterday. I prayed for her healing. It didn't come. I prayed for the rapture. It didn't come. Then I saw God's hand moving. Not in a month, but years later. God drew me what was flowing out of Martha during her last days. God's glory. (New Hope Publishers 2008)

Have you ever seen God at work?

Please share with group if you feel comfortable

Day 4
Somewhere

Psalm 31:9 "Be gracious O Lord, for I am in distress; my eye is wasted from grief...(NIV)

Somewhere

Somewhere along the path I lost my

Somewhere along the way lost my hope

Somehow without my hope I found resentment.

Somehow my resentment turned to anger.

Somehow my anger grew into bitterness

Somehow my bitterness flew into rage.

Somehow my rage consumed me.

Somewhere in the rage I blamed you,

O God

For all the Pain

For all of the abandonment.

For all the fear.

For all the injustices.

For all the loneliness

For all the sorrow.

For all the grief.

For all the sorrow.

For all the tears.

For all the dreams I never lived. For all the hopes left unfulfilled.

Do you know O God, how difficult this is for me?

To take your hand and trust you

In what I cannot see.

You know my past and pain so well,

For it is real to me.

Can you take my tattered life and help me love for eternity?

Somewhere along the road, O Lord,

I gave my heart.

Somewhere along the trodden path

I lost those that loved.

If I give you my honesty

And choose to do what is right,

Will you in turn give me the strength

To last the god and holy fight?

Because I come before you as a little child

So very very lost.

Somewhere along the way I blamed

You for all my pain and thus the cost.(Shameless New Hope Publishers, 2008)

Can you relate to this poem? Please tell why or why not.

Sometimes we don't know what is up and what is down. I felt so lost after Martha died. I got in a "rotational" It was healing to be around her kids. If I couldn't be around her, then the next best thing were her kids. When I looked at them I saw Martha.

I made a scrapbook for Martha's mom after Martha died. It was very healing to make it. I also ran the same marathon that Martha had run when she was just 3 months pregnant. Although I didn't have all the obstacles that Martha did, I still ran in memory of her. Jane, her mother, came to cheer me on, as did my sister. Running the marathon, was one of the greatest achievements of my life. Running it helped me in the grief process.

I believe that whatever it takes to heal, then, you just do the Nike slogan...just do it.You may not get the support that you need but you and God are a majority. Do it publically or privately. Healing takes action.

Read and record John 8:32

The word "to know" in the Greek means action. You can't just think something, you must put a plan into action. For example, I can mentally know I want to make an? A in Biology. But until I do something with that truth, then it will be an unfilled dream. I must put a plan into action and set time to do my work necessary for that.

Do you have any goals or dreams? If so what are they?

Dreams are goals that have been met or not yet met. What steps are you taking to meet those goals/dreams

Day 5
The Refining

Isaiah 48:10 "Behold I have refined you, but not as silver; I have tried you in the furnace of affliction." (NIV)

Sometimes

Sometimes this grief washes over me

Like the ocean waves crashing against the sand.

Unending. Ceaseless. Perpetual.

To the mere spectator turned vacationer

The water brings with it peace, solitude, and rest.

But to the resident who beaches upon

Its shore day after day and month after month,

The waves carry pain, loneliness, and grief.

How long, O Lord,

Will the waters captivate my life?

My every move. Thought. Response.

My world stopped while the world went rudely on.

My tears flowed unceasingly while others seemed to smile effortlessly.

Where is my hope O God?

Who is my avenger today, O Lord?

Why do these lips honestly confess the horrors of my heart?

For whatever is gone now

I can rest assured that

You are still in control,

And one day reveal the seemingly painful madness

Of the here and now,

To the overwhelmingly speechless perfection

Of your divine plain. Your method is perfect.

Your timing is perfect.

Your refining is perfect.

May this life of mine not tarry in vain

As I seek Your hand during this molding process.

(Debbie Vanderslice, Shameless, p. 80, 2008 New Hope Publishers)

Malachi 3:3

How does God get rid of our impurities?

Sometimes, not always, God uses hardships to get out our impurities. If everything was fine and we never struggled God could not use our trials and tribulations to mold us into what He wants us to become.

What hardships are you currently undergoing?

If someone never seems to struggle and says, "I'm so blessed" and she is currently undergoing a divorce she is missing God at work in her life. The particular woman I am thinking about a woman always says," I'm so blessed." She never shared any of her struggles either in a group or one on one. She was what I call a Christian fake. It is not if we will go through hardships but when.

Just look at Paul. He did not have a healthy and wealthy life. He suffered all sorts of hardships and yet he used those hardships to pen most of the New Testament.

Good can overcome bad any day. But with Christ, we will have to deal with disappointments, sickness, disease, ridicule, and the list goes on and on.

Disappoints will came our way. The real question is how will we react to them? We will go through the fire. Will we allow God to transform us in the fire?

Read Philippians 3:14what does it say?

Prayer: Dear God, help us to seek you even during the dark days. Help us keep our eyes on you and run to "win the prize." Give us the fortitude to not give up but to run the race God has planned just for us. May we all seek "the balm in Gilead" and seek God in all we do and say.

Write your own prayer in the space below

Printed in the United States
By Bookmasters